ONLINE TEACHING

THE MOST COMPLETE GUIDE ABOUT TEACHING ONLINE WITH GOOGLE CLASSROOM AND ZOOM MEETINGS. THREE BOOKS INCLUDED FOR THE BEST MODERN TEACHER.

RICHARD V. ROSS

RICHARD V. ROSS

© Copyright 2020 - All rights reserved.

The content contained within this book may not be reproduced, duplicated or transmitted without direct written permission from the author or the publisher. Under no circumstances will any blame or legal responsibility be held against the publisher, or author, for any damages, reparation, or monetary loss due to the information contained within this book. Either directly or indirectly.

Legal Notice

This book is copyright protected. This book is only for personal use. You cannot amend, distribute, sell, use, quote or paraphrase any part, or the content within this book, without the consent of the author or publisher.

Disclaimer Notice

Please note the information contained within this document is for educational and entertainment purposes only. All effort has been executed to present accurate, up to date, and reliable, complete information. No warranties of any kind are declared or implied. Readers acknowledge that the author is not engaging in the rendering of legal, financial, medical or professional advice. The content within this book has been derived from various sources. Please consult a licensed professional before attempting any techniques outlined in this book.

By reading this document, the reader agrees that under no circumstances is the author responsible for any losses, direct or indirect, which are incurred as a result of the use of information contained within this document, including, but not limited to, errors, omissions, or inaccuracies.

RICHARD V. ROSS

THIS BOOK INCLUDES

BOOK 1:

ONLINE TEACHING

The Complete Guide on How to Teach Effectively Online. Find Here the Best Strategies to Engage Your Students

BOOK 2:

GOOGLE CLASSROOM FOR TEACHERS
STEP BY STEP GUIDE

A Beginner's Guide to Google Classroom 2020 - 2021. Screenshots, Tips, And Tricks for The Best Modern Teacher. Including Pills of Mindset

BOOK 3:

ZOOM FOR TEACHERS STEP BY STEP GUIDE

A Beginner's Guide to Zoom 2020 – 2021. Screenshots, Tips and Tricks to Become the Best Modern Teacher.

ONLINE TEACHING

Table of Contents

INTRODUCTION **14**

CHAPTER 1: SURFACE BACKWARD DESIGN **18**

    MODELS 19
    DEFINING THE DESIRED RESULTS 20
    DECIDING PROOF OF DESIRED RESULTS 20
    PLANNING LEARNING MODULES AND EXPERIENCES 21
    PRINCIPLES 21
    SMALL TEACHING ONLINE QUICK TIP: SURFACE BACKWARD DESIGN ONLINE 23

CHAPTER 2: GUIDING LEARNING THROUGH ENGAGEMENT **26**

    WHAT IS YOUR CONSISTENT THEME? 26
    FUN BACKGROUNDS 28
    THE IMPORTANCE OF GOOD LIGHTING 28
    NO OUTSIDE DISTRACTIONS 29
    CREATE INTERACTIVE LEARNING ACTIVITIES 29
    CREATING A PLAN FOR YOUR ONLINE COURSES 30

CHAPTER 3: USING MEDIA AND TECHNOLOGY TOOLS **34**

    HARDWARE 34
    SOFTWARE 37

CHAPTER 4: BUILDING COMMUNITY **40**

    MODELS 40
    PRINCIPLES 41
    COMMUNITY BUILDING 101 42

CHAPTER 5: GIVING FEEDBACK **44**

    GETTING FEEDBACK FROM STUDENT 44
    REPLYING STUDENTS' FEEDBACK 46

CHAPTER 6: FOSTERING STUDENT PERSISTENCE AND SUCCESS **50**

    BUILD HIGHWAYS FOR STUDENT SUCCESS 50
    AVOID A CORRESPONDENCE COURSE 52
    AVOID WEEKEND DUE DATES 53
    PATHWAYS FOR YOUR SUCCESS 54

CHAPTER 7: CREATING AUTONOMY 56
- ACTIVE PARTICIPATION 56
- COLLABORATION AND COMMUNITY BUILDING 57
- AUTHENTIC ASSESSMENTS 58

CHAPTER 8: MAKING CONNECTIONS 60
- EFFECTIVE COMMUNICATION IN TEACHING 60
- UNDERSTANDING CODES 61
- THE NON-VERBAL CODE 63

CHAPTER 9: DEVELOPING AS AN ONLINE INSTRUCTOR 66
- DAILY PRACTICES TO BE AN EFFECTIVE ONLINE TEACHER 66
- TOP 5 QUALITIES OF EFFECTIVE ONLINE TEACHERS 68

CHAPTER 10: HOW TO ASSESS STUDENTS 72
- UTILIZING QUIZ 72
- FILL-IN-THE-BLANK CLOZE ACTIVITY METHOD 72
- MATCHING QUESTIONS 73
- FORUM POST 73
- PEER EVALUATION AND REVIEW 74
- POLL/QUIZ RESULTS IN REAL-TIME 74
- EXIT CARDS 74
- USING RUBRICS FOR ASSESSMENT 75
- UTILIZING TURNITIN 75

CHAPTER 11: CHAPTER 11: CRITICAL SKILLS TO TEACH THE FIRST WEEKS OF SCHOOL 78

CHAPTER 12: WAYS TO END A LESSON AND EXPECTATIONS 84
- HERE ARE 5 CREATIVE IDEAS FOR SUCCESSFULLY BRINGING YOUR LESSON TO A CLOSE 84
- PARENTAL EXPECTATIONS 86

CHAPTER 13: HOW TO MOTIVATE PUPILS 88

CONCLUSION 94

GOOGLE CLASSROOM FOR TEACHERS STEP BY STEP GUIDE

Table of Contents

INTRODUCTION **100**

    WHAT IS GOOGLE CLASSROOM? 100
    EVOLUTION OF GOOGLE CLASSROOM 100
    DOES GOOGLE CLASSROOM BECOME AN LMS? 102
    IS GOOGLE CLASSROOM FREE OF COST? 102
    IMPLEMENTATION AND INTEGRATION 102
    WHO IS ELIGIBLE FOR GOOGLE CLASSROOMS? 103
    GOOGLE CLASSROOMS SUPPORT SERVICE 103
    CAN THE CLASSROOM BE USED IF G SUITE FOR EDUCATION DOMAIN INCLUDES GMAIL DISABLED? 104
    COULD THE CLASSROOM BE USED IF G SUITE FOR EDUCATION DOMAIN HAS BEEN DISABLED? 104
    DIFFERENCE BETWEEN GOOGLE CLASSROOM AND GOOGLE ASSIGNMENT 104
    ACCESSING GOOGLE CLASSROOM FROM SCHOOL ACCOUNT AND PERSONAL ACCOUNT 105
    GOOGLE CLASSROOM FOR VISUALLY IMPAIRED PEOPLE 105
    GOOGLE CLASSROOM API OUTLINE 106

CHAPTER 1: THE MODERN TEACHER **108**

    RUN A VIRTUAL FIELD TRIP 108
    REVIEW FIELD TRIPS VIRTUALLY 109
    CALM A NOISY CLASSROOM 109
    USE VIDEOS FOR MINI-LESSONS 110
    CO-ORDINATE LIVE VIDEO 110
    PLAY PODCASTS 111
    ADD MULTIMEDIA ELEMENTS TO PRESENTATIONS 112
    SEND ADAPTIVE CONTENT 112
    OFFER AN ONLINE CLASS CALENDAR 113

CHAPTER 2: PILLS OF MINDSET **114**

CHAPTER 3: BENEFITS OF GOOGLE CLASSROOM **118**

    ACCESSIBILITY 118
    EXPOSURE 118
    PAPERLESS 119
    TIME SAVER 119

- COMMUNICATION 119
- COLLABORATE 119
- ENGAGEMENT 120
- DIFFERENTIATION 120
- FEEDBACK 120
- DATA ANALYSIS 120

CHAPTER 4: VIRTUAL CLASSES 122

- PREPARE YOUR MIND 122
- BEING FLEXIBLE IS KEY 122
- COMMUNICATE REGULARLY AND PROVIDE FEEDBACK 123
- HOW TO BE A VIRTUAL COMMUNICATOR? 123
- HOW DO TEACHERS COMMUNICATE VIRTUALLY? 124
- BE A BETTER VIRTUAL COMMUNICATOR 125

CHAPTER 5: GETTING STARTED WITH GOOGLE CLASSROOM 130

CHAPTER 6: NAVIGATE GOOGLE CLASSROOM 134

- NAVIGATION AND SOME OTHER SETTINGS OF GOOGLE CLASSROOM 134
- THE CLASSROOM HOMEPAGE 134
- GOOGLE CLASSROOM MENU 136
- HOW TO NAVIGATE YOUR CLASS? 137
- YOU CAN HANDLE OR CHANGE CLASS DETAILS 141
- EDIT A CLASS SECTION, NAME, ROOM, DESCRIPTION, OR SUBJECT 142
- RESET, COPY OR TURN OFF THE CLASS CODE 142
- CHOOSE HOW CLASSWORK NOTIFICATIONS SHOW ON THE STREAM PAGE 144
- TO NOTE DELETED STUDENT POSTS 144

CHAPTER 7: HOW TO SET-UP GOOGLE CLASSROOM 146

- CREATING AND SETTING CLASSES 146
- INVITING YOUR STUDENTS ON GOOGLE CLASSROOM 147
- HOW TO CREATE AND COLLECT ASSIGNMENTS/TASKS FROM STUDENTS 151
- HOW TO USE QUESTION 153
- HOW TO USE EVALUATION TOOL/RUBRICS 155
- USE STREAM 159
- COPY A COURSE 160

CHAPTER 8: HOW TO SET DUE DATE, MANAGE HOMEWORK, AND ASSIGNMENTS? 162

- ADD AN ASSIGNMENT 162
- CREATING AN ASSIGNMENT 162
- INPUTTING GRADE CATEGORY 163
- CHANGE THE POINT VALUE 163
- EDIT DUE DATE OR TIME 164

ADD A TOPIC	164
INSERT ATTACHMENTS	164
ADD A RUBRIC	167
POSTING, SCHEDULING, OR SAVING DRAFT ASSIGNMENT	171
TO REUSE ANNOUNCEMENT AND ASSIGNMENT	173
RESPONSE AND RETURN OF GRADES	175

CHAPTER 9: DIFFERENCE BETWEEN GOOGLE CLASSROOM AND OTHER PLATFORMS 176

THE HARDWARE DIFFERENCES	176
GOOD FOR LOWER LEVEL GRADES	177
GOOGLE CLASSROOM FOCUSES ON ORGANIZATION	177
APPLE CLASSROOM HAS MORE INTERACTIVE LESSONS	177
GOOGLE CLASSROOM ALLOWS FOR MULTIPLE DEVICES TO BE USED	178
YOU DON'T HAVE TO CHOOSE	179

CHAPTER 10: BEST EXTENSIONS FOR BOTH TEACHERS & STUDENTS 180

GRAMMAR & SPELLING TOOLS	180
LANGUAGE TOOL	181
PLAGIARISM CHECKERS	182
STAY FOCUSED	184

CHAPTER 11: TIPS AND TRICKS 188

TIPS FOR TEACHERS	188
TIPS FOR STUDENTS	190

CHAPTER 12: FAQS ABOUT GOOGLE CLASSROOM 194

IS IT EASY TO GET STARTED WITH GOOGLE CLASSROOM?	194
HOW ARE APPS FOR EDUCATION AND CLASSROOM CONNECTED?	194
DOES IT COST TO USE GOOGLE CLASSROOM?	195
CAN I STILL USE CLASSROOM IF IT IS DISABLED ON MY DOMAIN?	195
DO I NEED TO HAVE GMAIL ENABLED TO USE CLASSROOM?	196
WILL I HAVE TO WORK WITH ADS ON GOOGLE CLASSROOM?	196

CHAPTER 13: PROS & CONS OF USING GOOGLE CLASSROOM 198

PROS	198
CONS	199
GOOGLE CLASSIFICATION TEACHING QUALITY	200

CONCLUSION 202

ZOOM FOR TEACHERS STEP BY STEP GUIDE

Table of Contents

INTRODUCTION **208**

CHAPTER 1: INTRODUCTION TO ZOOM CLOUD MEETING **210**
- WHAT IS ZOOM? 210
- HOW DOES ZOOM WORK? 212
- DIFFERENCE BETWEEN FREE ZOOM AND PAID ZOOM 214
- ZOOM SECURITY UPDATES AND ISSUES 215
- TROUBLESHOOTING 216

CHAPTER 2: APP INSTALLATION **222**
- GETTING STARTED WITH ZOOM 222
- ZOOM MAIN FEATURES 233

CHAPTER 3: ZOOM FOR TEACHERS **244**
- ENGAGING STUDENTS USING DIFFERENT FEATURES 253
- LIVE STREAM A MEETING WITH ZOOM 264
- TIPS FOR LIVE STREAM ZOOM 266

CHAPTER 4: HOW TO USE ZOOM FOR WEBINARS **268**
- ZOOM HAS TAKEN THE LEAD IN MAKING THESE ACTIVITIES POSSIBLE ... 269
- SCHEDULING A WEBINAR 275
- CONFIGURING POLLS 278

CONCLUSION **280**

ONLINE TEACHING

THE COMPLETE GUIDE ON HOW TO TEACH EFFECTIVELY ONLINE. FIND HERE THE BEST STRATEGIES TO ENGAGE YOUR STUDENTS

RICHARD V. ROSS

Introduction

Online teaching is not something new as it has been in existence for many decades. However, its technology came not too long ago. The idea behind it has always been in existence as far back as 170 years ago. The origin of online teaching and education is in a correspondence course that was being offered in the UK. In the course, the instructor will send lessons to students and receive their assignments through mails.

Then, it was considered as distance learning. It was this idea that propelled the modern idea of online teaching. Online learning gives room for students to interact with one another, and this creates another classroom, which is virtual. One of the primary goals of education is the promotion of life-long learning. This means that education must always motivate people to want to learn and gather knowledge. Even outside school, students should be interested in learning.

It is now the sole responsibility of teachers to make an effort to develop learning among their students. They can do this by setting up effective classroom management, which researchers have found out to be essential in the process of maximizing the learning abilities of students by teachers. The creation of an intranet by the University of Illinois for students in 1960 was the first move that launched the surfacing of online teaching in modern ways.

The intranet was designed to help students gain access to online materials and listen to recorded lectures. Intranet later evolved into PLATO, which means: Programmed Logic for Automatic Teaching Operations. PLATO gained a global reach operating in various terminals. It was later used to develop many of the social networking features, such as chat rooms, message boards, screen sharing, etc. that we now use today. Right from the creation of the intranet, many other institutions worked tirelessly to promote online learning. The result is what we currently have today with a lot of online tools made available for teaching and learning online.

However, there have been many opinions from educators and teachers against the use of the internet to teach. One of the educators that spoke vehemently against the use of online teaching is Mark Edmundson, a professor of English at the University of Virginia. In his opinion, he claimed that teachers need to see their students physically to understand their physical, emotional, and intellectual needs. This is what will help the teacher to know how best to help them. He further claimed that teaching is dialogic. And this is what allows students to grasp the ideas explained in each class easily. For Mark, online teaching is in monologue, and it is a one-size-fits-all approach to teaching, which is not adequate. He emphasized on the need to create a community of learning between teachers and their students.

Nonetheless, there are several reasons for adopting online learning, especially in a period of an epidemic like this. The presence of the coronavirus ravaging our world has revealed another reason for online teaching. Aside from other reasons for adopting the online means of education, the undesirable isolation that we are presently going through necessitates the need for its global adoption. Generally, teaching online has the following benefits:

It Creates time flexibility: Online teaching makes learning easy. It creates flexibility in time for both the teacher and the students. Students can easily learn at their productive hours. It allows students to approach learning based on their pace by following a certain framework designed for the study. Also, flexibility is reflected in the easiness of breaking the syllabus down into smaller units that the students can easily learn.

Increased location flexibility: Students can now learn without necessarily being confined in their classrooms. Even the teacher can set up his or her lectures in the comfort of his or her room. These benefits help to achieve a goal of education—to promote life-long education. Despite the isolation and school closure policies, which serve as measures against the deadly coronavirus, students can still learn as much as they would have learned in their classrooms.

It creates a practical context: By learning online, students will begin to see novel relevance to their contemporary society. They will start to gain access to professional and industrial practices, which is one thing they need outside of school.

It eases the process of Information Sharing: Both students and teachers can now share information easily and readily. They will also gain access to more information by joining other online learning platforms. This makes learning more practicable.

It provides enriching and diverse experience: Learning online enhances students' experience. It does this by providing them with opportunities to collaborate across disciplines and cultures. This learning opportunities can occur at both the local and national levels.

There are many more reasons we should adopt online teaching. At present, it will help to cater for the lack of contact learning we are supposed to be having ongoing in schools. Rather than making students go for months without any educational activity. It is best to bring them to the virtual learning space where they will gain a lot and get themselves prepared for the real world.

CHAPTER 1:

Surface Backward Design

Backward design takes a holistic approach to the process of learning, and it encourages you as an instructor to focus on how learning exercises and assessments ensure that the course objectives are achieved. Backward design allows teachers to figure out which materials are essential for students to achieve the expressed learning goals. This is easier for you to choose what to add to the learning curriculum and what to leave out. It is also making the learning process more productive as your students would be able to focus on the things that really matter. It is easier for you to determine the ideal student learning results, evaluate these results and determine the classroom exercises and related course materials that are expected to obtain these results. Another advantage of using backward design is that student's value less complicated learning. When you share course objectives clearly with your students, they will understand what is expected of them and work towards achieving these objectives. Teaching using backward design gives both the students and instructors greater clarity.

When designing a course, there are three important questions you need to ask yourself to ensure that you are following backward design approach. These questions are:

> 1. What should my students be able to do at the end of the course? This address learning goals and objectives for the course.

> 2. How will I measure if my students can do that? This enables you to develop a streamlined method of assessment.

3. How will I get my students ready for the assessment? This enables you put together a teaching plan or curriculum.

Creating great learning objectives through clear statements that tell your students the skills and knowledge they are expected to have at the end of the course is the first step in the backward design process.

The next step is determining how you will measure their skills and knowledge based on the learning objectives you have created. Whatever method of assessment you pick should be appropriate for the course and tailored to clearly show their understanding of the important parts of what they are learning. Also, each assessment you give should be suited to their level. For example, if the topic you are creating an assessment for is an introductory level topic, its objectives are bound to concentrate on remembering past knowledge, understanding the basic concepts of the new topic, and linking past knowledge to the basic concepts of the new topic. As such, assignments and tests that focus on asking students to remember old knowledge, answering questions about basic concepts, and linking both old knowledge and the new basic concepts together, are appropriate.

Finally, you can now design streamlined training modules for the course. Your training modules should be custom fitted to guarantee that students are prepared for assessments. Your teaching modules should also be engaging because the more engaged your students are, the more chances they will have to learn.

Models

Backward design approach has three stages. These stages are defining the desired results, deciding proof of desired results, and planning learning modules and experiences.

Defining the Desired Results

The big picture that you feel is important for your students to have regardless of whether they remember anything else from your course or not is what we are discussing here. This big picture can stand out from the vast range of information you think the students should have about the topic or course. The big picture is the focal point your students need to understand. Without this big picture, the course, module, or other learning material would be pointless.

How to define the desired outcomes:

    1. Identify the big picture.

    2. Concentrate on the big picture.

Deciding Proof of Desired Results

Assessment is the invisible finish line on your students' "race" to learning. It is what proves that both you and your students have reached the finish line of the particular topic or course and that everyone has achieved the specified objectives. It is up to you to estimate out what that finish line will be. What is sufficient proof of your students' understanding and mastery of the topic or course? Is it getting at least 70% or 80% in an assessment test or as a grand total in a group of assessment exercises including tests, an examination, gradable term papers, and group projects?

How to decide proof of desired results:

    1. Decide satisfactory levels of proof that showing you and your students have reached the ideal outcomes.

    2. Create finish line assessment tests and a range of evaluation techniques (assignments, tests, projects, and so on.)

Planning Learning Modules and Experiences

When you are planning and designing your instructional materials, there are a few elements you should consider. You should structure your learning modules and learning experiences in a way that allows your students to know how each learning material is related to the general objective, how it expands on their earlier information, and what is required of them to successfully finish the module and show mastery of the learning materials. The learning modules or experiences should also be related to their interest or be flexible enough for them to personalize it. In conclusion, the direction you pick should give your students chances to gain mastery of the course and to review their own growth.

How to plan learning modules and experiences:

1. Design exercises that will cause desired outcomes to occur.

2. Focus on information and skills that students should acquire to have the ideal outcomes.

Principles

One of the fundamental objectives of designing learning situations using backward design learning principles is to deliver learning experiences that are suitable for your students. Ideally, the learning conditions you create should be flexible and should allow all your students to take part in the learning process in ways that address their issues.

By giving students alternatives in learning and exhibition of their learning, you place emphasis on a flexibility that supports a mixed range of learning material as opposed to just sticking to what one textbook or reading material says. This way, your students will have a better chance at learning because the materials they choose are suited to cater to their learning needs. When relying primarily on traditional teaching methods and following textbooks' letters, your alternatives (in learning materials and exercises) are frequently constrained to what the book offers. However, when teaching for understanding, you are just constrained by what your students should achieve before the end of the teaching session. When you use backward design learning principles, your students have alternatives by the way they learn, how they convey what they have learned, and furthermore how they modify their learning to accommodate their personal interests and learning goals.

Teaching towards understanding of the big picture rather than basically covering the material out of a picked course material gives you greater flexibility and gives your students more chances to learn. This is the focal principle of backward design. Backward design encourages students to concentrate on, and connect with, the learning objectives.

This brings us to another key principle of Backward Design: planning. To successfully use the backward design structure, you need to plan your objectives. If you want your students to leave the learning session with a good understanding of the big picture and key ideas, you need to factor in enough time into your course for them to connect and relate with the major ideas in different ways. Spend more time with them on the major ideas and less time on the minor ideas.

Another principle of backward design is that it enables you to ask (and answer) some significant questions concerning your students' learning. These questions include:

- Is the learning module I created impactful, or is it just strong enough to catch my students' interest briefly?
- How will I know that my pupils have gained an understanding of the subject matter?

Using the backward design structure is like embarking on a journey. At the start of your journey, the goal at the top of your priority list is your destination and you need to figure out a schedule that allows you get there. You also need to design metrics that allow you to judge if you have gotten to your destination or not. It is as simple as this.

Regardless of whether you are designing a talk, an entire course, or some other instructional material, you can use Backward Design principles to assist you with staying on target while addressing the greatest questions that your students will need you to answer in due order regarding what you are teaching: "what really matters?"

Small Teaching Online Quick Tip: Surface Backward Design Online

In terms of small teaching online, backward design is one of the best ways to break down online teaching into small bits that can make it easier for you to teach students in ways that will have long-lasting effects. Backward design online follows the general steps for traditional physical learning.

Step 1 – Identify Desired Outcomes

In doing this, some important questions need to be posed. These questions include:

> 1. What would you like your students to take home from the teaching?

> 2. What is the desired result or aim of each lesson and of the overall learning plan?

In this case, let us say you are teaching a course on nutrition. The three focal points of a course on nutrition are understanding concepts about nutrition, understanding how people can get the most nutrition out of their meals, and understanding eating patterns.

Using the aforementioned questions, you will most likely arrive at a desired outcome like this: At the tip of the course, pupils should be able to use their knowledge of nutrition to design meals that enable them and others to get the best nutrition taking different eating patterns into consideration.

Step 2 – Determine Worthy Proof

It is not just sufficient to identify the outcome you want. You need to have a measurement system that allows you to identify worthy proof that the desired outcome has been achieved. Tests and assignments can be great measurement systems.

Using the aforementioned example, a worthy proof would be a test in which the students put together a one-week meal plan for a family making use of the lessons they have been taught. The objective is a delicious and healthy meal plan.

Step 3 – Plan Learning Encounters and Guidance

As an instructor, you should first consider the skills and knowledge your students will require so as to complete the assessment test or assignment.

Based on the aforementioned example, students would need to be informed about various nutritional categories, human nutrition requirements (proteins, carbohydrates, sugars, minerals, vitamins and so on.), and about what food sources give these requirements.

Your teaching techniques should include personal one-on-one communication between you and your students and inductive strategies, as well as group exercises which can be done through online platforms like Zoom.

CHAPTER 2:

Guiding Learning through Engagement

Education is migrating online at warp speed. Preparing your virtual classroom is a relatively new topic that many educators need to spend time on. A virtual classroom is a term used to describe everything students interact with online, including the videos they watch and the online tests that they take. For many teachers, their virtual classroom encompasses the background scene for their recorded videos, and the engagement strategies that they use to encourage students to learn.

The idea of a virtual classroom, spans beyond your regularly scheduled virtual office hours and therefore it includes each touchpoint students interact within your online learning offering. Teachers who can transform the best parts of their classroom into a virtual environment will be able to give students new and improved ways of learning. Here are some helpful tips to keep in mind while planning your virtual classroom.

What Is Your Consistent Theme?

Consistency is key to creating a cohesive virtual classroom experience for students. Consider the elements of your classroom that make it special and different. How can these translate into a virtual classroom? Maybe you can take a picture of your physical classroom and use it as a virtual background.

Have you ever considered the power of colors in education? Colors can be used to imply deeper meaning to students and support your lessons in ways that other forms of communication cannot.

Here is a list of colors and the emotions that they can be used to invoke.

1. **Blue:** This can be used to set a calm and serene stage for your students. Blue is the color of the sky, and it can be associated with a sense of tranquility. Warm blue tones can be used in your lessons theme to create calmness which can offset stressful situations or content.

2. **Orange:** Orange is an exciting color. It can be used in energetic ways to convey new ideas and information. Orange is generally associated with citrus fruits and therefore can convey health and energy. It is a great color to use to help spark creativity and give your lessons a sense of adventure.

3. **Yellow:** Yellow is a joyous color that is fun and happy. This is the color of the sun and it's therefore friendly and comforting. Yellow can be used to convey happy thoughts but be careful about using it too frequently. Some shades of yellow are used for caution signs because it can be alarming.

4. **Green:** Green is the color of growth. Green can be used very powerfully when used in association with money. Green also represents nature and life in the world outdoors. In general, green is a color that stimulates movement and energy. There are many shades of green which can vary in meaning. Light shades of green are youthful, and they can bring a sense of energy to your lessons. Darker shades of this color can convey a sense of wellbeing and permanency.

Perhaps you can find a few images or color schemes that can be used consistently throughout your online materials. There is a great website called colorcombos.com that you can use to find exciting color combinations to use in your classroom. Take some time to plan out your theme so that it will be instantly recognizable to your students. You can include these colors and themes in your virtual backgrounds, on slides, quizzes, assessments, and video content.

Fun Backgrounds

Whether it is a virtual or real background, make it fun and creative. The more vibrant your background is, the easier it will be for your students to stay engaged and connected. Check out what some of the top YouTube influencers are doing and see just how easy it is to position yourself against a fun background. Consider putting pictures on the wall, using a colored light, or a green screen. Maybe you can even place a living thing in your background like a fishbowl or a plant. Imagine how fun it would be to refer to your pet fish at the start of each class.

Your background does not have to be spectacular or extravagant, but something as simple as a dash of color, some interesting props or a virtual classroom background will do the trick to set the tone of the class. Paying attention to your background shows that you care, and it can become a topic of casual conversation as you upgrade, rotate, and change your background. You can use physical objects in your background as icebreakers and conversation starters.

The Importance of Good Lighting

Good lighting has a major impact when it comes to planning your virtual classroom. You want students to see you easily and you want to avoid looking scary. Yes, the software and equipment you use can dictate the output. Lighting is a key ingredient for making your video content successful.

Try testing your video to ensure that your face is not too light or too dark. Position yourself near a window or move the lighting around in your room. A few simple adjustments can make a big difference. Record a few sample videos clips from different angles and play them back.

Which one looked the best? You can try to alter the angle of your webcam or tilting your laptop screen if your webcam is built-in. Simple adjustments make a big difference.

No Outside Distractions

Be mindful of outside distractions during your time online. If your apartment is on a busy street where traffic is constantly driving by, those noises (beeps and vrooms) can really take away from your lesson. Outside noises are distracting, and they can break the attention of your students. To fix this, make sure you set up your virtual classroom in a quiet space where you can close windows and doors to reduce unwanted noise. You may want to put a sign on your door that lets your family and friends know when you are recording a video.

Create Interactive Learning Activities

In a traditional classroom, it's relatively easy to plan a learning activity and tell students to push their desks together and collaborate on an assignment. But in a virtual setting, you will need to learn how to use new tools for small group collaboration. Consider coming up with a few ideas that are relevant to your lesson and that will genuinely promote genuine interaction. For example, you can start with some classic ice-breaker exercises such as "if you were stranded on an island, what would be one thing you would bring?" You can adapt classic ice-breaker exercises to fit your classroom. For example, "If you had to take the mid-term exam tomorrow, what is one book you would bring?" This will help encourage conversation between students and helps them to feel more involved, even at a distance.

During your first couple of interactive learning exercises consider starting with ice-breaker questions that will allow your class to get to know each other. Then you can use small group breakout rooms and take a large classroom and divide students into smaller groups. In small breakout groups, you can decide to randomly assign students into a specific group size, or manually place students into small groups of your choosing. As the teacher, you can broadcast questions to all small groups to give them questions to work on together.

Creating a Plan for Your Online Courses

Having a plan in place for your online course is essential. Start with an outline and complete it with detailed information for each major lesson. Planning an online course requires a focus on digital assets that will enrich your presentations. These assets will be recorded and uploaded to your learning management system. Therefore, the way you think about preparing your online course will include a variety of media and use some of the technology.

Think about flipping your classroom when you are planning an online course. In a traditional classroom, students would listen to the lecture or presentation, and then do the homework at home. But with a flipped classroom, it's the other way around for reasons that we have already explained. In a nutshell, this is an instructional method that combines both student engagement and active learning styles with online learning. As a result, it gives students the ability to digest your online course content at their own pace. Your online course should be presented in such a way that students receive clear guidance and clarity about the learning objectives.

Considerations for Online Courses

1. **Provide Students with the Benefits:** At the beginning of your online course, share what your students will learn from the course. Review the learning outcomes and let students know how their

investment in learning will positively impact them. You can enrich your storytelling capabilities with success stories, short video clips, and images that resemble the successful outcomes that you want students to visualize. In the end, they should be excited about learning and see a logical, sequenced flow for the course.

2. **Videos vs. Live Sessions:** Go through your lessons and separate them into two different categories: lower-order targets, and higher-order objectives. As a rule of thumb, the things that will require more exploration, demonstration, and discussion should be live sessions. Use your pre-recorded video lessons to review core concepts and fundamentals. Think about your videos as time spent with students, where they can pause what they are learning and do research. Therefore, you can enclose a lot of ground and cover in-depth research assignments inside your videos. Then you can use upcoming sessions to further review the content students learned from the recorded videos they watched.

3. **Nailing Down Activities:** Take some time to research activities you can do with students to keep them interested and connected. For instance, for a science topic, would experiments be better, or a group project? Think about activities having multiple starting points. Perhaps you talk about an upcoming activity in your recorded videos and share some successful outcomes from a previous class. Then you can try the activities in a virtual classroom setting and take things further in small breakout groups.

4. **Collaboration and Feedback:** How will you and your students collaborate? Will it be via live Zoom sessions or a specific journaling exercise? Consider asking students if they enjoyed or found the activity helpful. Ask your students to provide non-verbal feedback with a thumb up or a thumb down. Assign students projects to collaborate on using your LMS system. Students may

also suggest their own online collaboration methods and submit their progress each week.

5. **Keep it Colorful:** No one, especially students, want to watch a dull, boring, and lifeless video. Make your slides colorful and be creative to keep students' attention. This is especially helpful for visual learners. Consider including popular memes and slides with a joke or two to make students laugh.

6. **Do Not Forget About Parents:** Incorporate time to update parents in your plan. Having the support and input of parents is critical for a successful online course. Parents need to know what their children are learning and how they are learning.

RICHARD V. ROSS

CHAPTER 3:

Using Media and Technology Tools

The assets you might want for encouraging on the web resemble some other assets in educating: everything relies upon what your students' request. On the occasion that you sign in with focus that initiates online instructors, whether, for business English classes or groups of youthful students, your customer can give you a thought of what videoconferencing programming bundle they have to utilize. Balanced students probably won't be so prescriptive, yet as their educator, you should have the option to utilize whatever equipment and programming bundle meets their wants. Actually, you'll in all probability end up being an IT guide, when the sign bombs on the application they force utilizing!

Hardware

A Stable Internet Connection

In the event that it's not instructing granny to suck eggs, you won't save your online understudies for long on the off chance that you must desert exercises because of the association down. Unmistakably, what considers quality changes wide over the world, be that as it may, talk with your net provider about an approach to expand the speed of the administration, for example, by utilizing a PC with a link snared to the switch, rather than Wi-Fi?

Your students can resolve to go to exercises from anyplace. You can make them stroll from the work environment to the metro and sitting on a noncurrent elevator in a strip mall–any way you can't escape with

pag. 34

things like that as an instructor. Those photos of the online instructor doing it from a lawn chair by the Caribbean are somewhat implausible. Your steady web association should be in an exceptionally calm, sufficiently bright, proficient looking spot. You'll moreover need a back-up plan for once the web will go down, which can occur. The information on your portable no doubt isn't consistent (or modest) enough to continue entire exercises. However, it'll accomplish for correspondence along with your understudies in a crisis.

A Variety of Devices: PC, Laptop, Tablet, and Smartphone

Truly, every one of them. The best-case circumstance is to do the entirety of your classes on a PC, furnishing you with generally potential to perform various tasks and access assets both on the web and in your ever-growing materials organizer previously and through exercises. This could be your set-up for your fundamental 'classroom' at home. Despite how shrewd touchscreen gadgets are turning into, there's no counterpart for a PC in a perfect world with an enormous screen, or perhaps two screens, so you'll keep a watch on your understudy constantly, even though opening and sharing various things.

Despite of the fact that the needs of our understudies are the start, center, and ultimate objective of all that we tend to do, remember to put your own working conditions first. When you work for an association, they need a risk to ensure that your working environment is pleasant for your stance, that you are permitted ordinary breaks, and that you have someone to address about movement wellbeing. None of this can be done for you once you're performing from home, and you neglect them at your danger. Try not to do your exercises round-sponsored over a PC shut at a little cell phone screen. It's not keen on you.

Having said that, its merits having those various gadgets as a back-up or for those events once you're in development, and you realize the web signal will be dependable enough to work, for example, at your mom's home.

Headphones and a Microphone

Try not to accept any gadget's inbuilt amplifier and speakers, since these can turn outcry adjust and be incredibly successful at discovering foundation signal, which can be diverting for your understudies. As a rule, this can be explicitly what they will utilize, and it'll be an occupation to tune in to and see them. Therefore, earphones that completely spread your ears can help you colossally. To give them the best likelihood of getting you, abstain from utilizing in-ear earphones with a mouthpiece bolster mostly down the lead, since this will rub against your wear and make you extreme to tune in to. Get the receiver as close to your mouth as could be expected under the circumstances.

A (Detachable) Digital Camera

Albeit most gadgets have a magnificently sufficient inbuilt webcam, the set-up recommended above to be utilized in many exercises the PC doesn't tend to, so you'll have to introduce one. Dislike the issues of sound. The understudy just must have the option to see you unmistakably–however, not in Hollywood-level top-notch in this manner, in case you're worried about the financial plan, you really don't need to stress over going first class here. Clearly, attempt before you buy in the event that you'll have the option to, and check what you resemble by doing a check call with a companion and getting them to record what they see.

Research how adaptable your advanced camera is regarding moving it around the region. In case you're showing youthful students, you would perhaps wish to do a lot of Total Physical Response, or just make them move and jump in regards to with them to keep them locked in. In addition, leaving aside the instruction hypothesis, in light of a legitimate concern for your stance, you may stay away from long stretches of succeeding sitting by remaining standing for a few or the entirety of your group time.

This has suggestions for what your understudy sees, so have various spots to put your webcam, all together that you'll have the option to do that.

Software

Note that we're not supporting any product bundle or the inverse. The ensuing depends on what understudies by and large wish or need to utilize, and some reflection on how supportive they're for instructing. You'll get a free form of its vast majority; however, the little speculation of a paid bundle can furnish you with a great deal of potential.

Skype and Different Videoconferencing Software System, E.G., Zoom

Skype has become the go-to programming bundle for video conferencing and is, at present, even an action word for its general concept! Generally, coordinated understudies can hope to utilize it, a base to begin with, so in case you're curious about Skype, play with the settings, realize how to shift the amplifier input which can supernaturally change for no evident explanation between one call and another advise yourself with what every single catch and symbol does, basically just on the off chance that the understudy doesn't comprehend and you need to talk them through something, such as offering their screen to you.

Zoom could be a savvy option, and much better for doing very discourse and making straightforward content notes. There's a whiteboard in the screen-sharing decisions that all members can expound on, and a 'break-out room' office where the educator will put understudies into little groups.

Note that you'll require a paid record to make class-length brings with more than each understudy in turn, however for balanced reasons for existing, there's no such limitation.

Voice Calling/Messaging Apps for Mobile-Use Only

As referenced in the equipment area, a lot of understudies can do their exercises on their telephone, and for the most part, the sign essentially works preferably on one stage over another. Despite the fact that you believe that you perceive an approach to utilize them, look online at what video instructional exercises people have made: you'll ceaselessly find something important. Did you know, perhaps, that you just can make a WhatsApp approach your telephone while furthermore utilizing WhatsApp web to give composing directing or mistake revision by means of the visit box on your work area!

Remember that a few nations square-bound programming framework, so an understudy in China will likely need to utilize WeChat, while someone inside the UAE will request that you use BOTIM. They could even have bought an exceptional form of this product bundle uniquely for the classes and can anticipate that educators should do likewise. You needn't have a full set-up of applications arranged from the very beginning; however, you'll doubtlessly understand that the more up to date your cell phone, there is a plenitude of decisions you'll have the option to offer your understudies.

A Cloud Account—Google Drive or OneDrive

One simple, free approach to put a whiteboard inside the online room is to possess a common archive open, any place you and your understudy can both compose all through the exercise and all things considered, they will save it for reference, or maybe do their homework on that. In case you're working with a gathering, it's a useful stage for peer coordinated effort, as well.

Sound editing software package, e.g., Audacity

Recollect once language classes utilized tapes? I shiver to assume what bands my own language educators bounced through in class, just to do an essential substance detail listening cycle. Nowadays, when showing on the web, it's entirely expected to utilize online assets, as BBC News recordings, which can, obviously, contend directly from the flexibly all through the exercise. On the chances that you might want to be extra adaptable or work on sub-abilities like transcription, you should record them independently and separate clasps. Daringness is free and very sufficient for this and works with the conventional console alternate ways for things like reordering; subsequently, you'll get to grasps with it rapidly.

A Video Camera

This is less basic. However, you may wish to make your own video substance to be utilized in school, send video headings to understudies for schoolwork, or record a video introduction for your site profile, a customary camera is going to preferred quality over a webcam for this (cameras on cell phones are fine).

Video Editing Software

You unquestionably don't need this to begin out, however along with your business-advancement cap on, concede all the recordings that return up once you Google 'web-based educating' or once understudies Google 'IELTS tips,' or regardless. To advance yourself, later on, you'll be all over YouTube and furthermore the like, and the slicker you look, the more hits (and clients) you'll get. You can start by making some clear exercise material joining a video of yourself giving headings cut with pictures, music, or designs.

CHAPTER 4:

Building Community

In the cutting-edge virtual class, students are not just the uninvolved beneficiaries of the course material and instructor's ability. Student expectations include considering the course content, submitting reactions to review questions, remarking on course mates' postings, driving class conversations, investment in synergistic group projects, and getting feedback from the instructor.

All in all, how is a community of students built in an online course? What are the attributes and practices? Teaching an online course is more than sitting in front of a computer. Connecting with individual students is important for a great learning. There are models that can be used to build online communities in which instructors and students participate fully.

Models

You can encourage students to contact colleagues with similar living conditions as the initial step to building connections in the online learning situation. Individual students could be partners in the same area of specialization or students from different backgrounds taking a necessary general course. Students can also build their own communities from online courses. Ask them to get acquainted with their colleagues, based on shared interests or work experience. Or if they are students in the same part of the country as each other, they can get together face to face. Let them know that taking an online class doesn't mean they need to take it in confinement. Encourage them to search each other out and make connections. These connections did not just furnish them with individuals to bounce thoughts off when working through their assignments, but they may also find that these individuals can assist them with understanding a topic or getting through a program. A large portion of the connections inside the learning community come through conversation sheets. This may also be the place students begin to build connections with each other. You can also show them how to intentionally read each other's conversation posts and catch up with extra examining questions prompting a better conversation and discussion. Be liberal and tolerating of varying conclusions or understandings. When you cannot help disagreeing with somebody, you should communicate your disagreement respectfully in a way that helps them get better. Reacting mindfully and respectfully to conversation posts can help build connections.

A simple answer like "I concur" or "Valid statement" or "You don't know what you are talking about" is adding zero to the learning experience of the community. Driving class conversations and doing your part for group projects are also approaches to build a community of students.

Principles

Principles need to be attached to the process of building online communities to ensure that these communities are the most beneficial for everyone involved.

Below are some of these principles.

> 1. Make posts that are on the subject and applicable to the course material.
>
> 2. Review and correct your posts before sending them.
>
> 3. Be as brief as possible while still offering a comprehensive statement.

4. Continuously give legitimate credit while referencing or citing another source.

5. Read all the messages in a thread before answering.

Community Building 101

Here are four of the more accessible ways that you can begin building community in your online course:

1. Keep Doing What You're Doing

Instructor modeling is the most important factor in creating a learning community. Your weekly emails, your encouraging remarks to students, your feedback on assignments, and your participation in the course discussions all go a long way in modeling the kind of interaction that's so crucial to for a true learning community.

2. Affirmation Goes a Long Way

Encouragement creates an atmosphere, and it builds a positive sense of community in your course. Catch your students doing something right. Try emailing particular students who have been active in the current week's discussion, and let them know that you appreciate how they are interacting with their group. Oftentimes, students will share personal stories in their posts. Encourage students who demonstrate this kind of openness because it invites other students to be their true selves online.

3. Share Your Life

Share stories from your own experience. Reflect on your own journey in your discipline, what your freshman year was like, where you made mistakes, and what you wish you would have known back then. Share your weaknesses. A wise professor who I've had the privilege to work with explained that. He said, "People admire you for your strength, but they connect with your vulnerability." As well, share from the present. Take time in your weekly emails or screencasts to share a bit about yourself, what you are reading, or what you're learning (of course, be brief and appropriate with what you share). This kind of immediacy sets the tone for the kind of communication you want to characterize your course.

4. Redesign an Assignment

Sometimes an assignment intended to leverage the power of a learning community just doesn't work, and we need to redesign it.

CHAPTER 5:

Giving Feedback

Instructors provide two types of feedback in the classroom to encourage students for higher performance; these are corrective and motivational feedback. Corrective feedback lets students know how well they perform on assignments, quizzes, projects, or class discussions. Motivational feedback helps students to complete tasks and work harder in order to achieve higher performance. In the face-to-face learning environment, students could walk into the professors' office to clarify confusing concepts if they have questions on their assignments. In the virtual classroom, students don't have such luxury. Students can only communicate by technology, and if a professor doesn't respond within a reasonable timeline, students are likely to repeat the same mistake on the next assignment. Education institutions usually have policies on the timeframe that instructors should respond to students in the virtual classroom. For general questions, they expect instructors to respond within 24 hours during the week and 72 hours on weekends. Feedback on graded assignments could take up to a week, depending on the assignment criteria. It is then the students' responsibility to follow up if they haven't heard from their instructors within a reasonable timeline.

Getting Feedback from Student

That is a broad topic that is very challenging for teachers. It is not only for online teachers but also for offline teachers. Feedback is a way that students access your works. It can be in the form of a survey or comments. How will you get feedback from your students?

Pre–Course Surveys or Questionnaires

Give the students the avenue to voice out their opinion throughout the course. Ask students questions like:

- What are their expectations about the learning experience?
- What interests them about the course?
- How they plan to utilize the knowledge, they will acquire from the course?
- What is there major fear about the course?
- What previous experience they have about the course?

Allow the students to include their names on the questionnaire during submission.

It will give you the avenue to know the expectation of each student towards the course.

Build Feedback Loops within the Course

You can build feedback loops like Quizzes within the course. It will help you to track the performance of each student.

If you discover that any of your students are lagging, you develop a plan of bringing him back on track.

There are certain areas that most students will be lagging in your course. In other to find such areas, ask students to complete a feedback form or survey.

Mix the survey with open-ended multiple-choice questions. Use online tools to provide anonymity so that the students will be frank.

Feedback Team

You can divide your students into various teams for feedback purposes. These students will work with you and the students to develop a tranquil learning environment. It is very good for offline tutors.

Post Course Individual Conversations

At the end of each lecture, you can create time to talk to each student or group of students that represents the class. Give them the guidelines ahead of the discussions so that they will know the type of questions to ask you. Allow them to express their opinion about the course. That will also help you to understand the areas that your students are not understanding.

Replying Students' Feedback

Getting feedback from students might be easy for you, but responding to most of that feedbacks might be challenging. Why? Because most of those feedbacks might require in-depth research from you. Like I said earlier, to be the best, you must read and reread. It is when you read that you get fresh ideas about the topic.

There are processes that you might need to follow when replying to students' feedback. But before we dive into that, you need to;

Set Clear Expectation

Set clear expectations at the beginning of your course. When designing your course, meditate on what the students will achieve from your course. Setting clear expectations will give the students a better idea about the course. It will save you the stress of receiving irrelevant feedbacks from students.

Let's look at how to reply to student feedback;

Be Cautious When Giving Student Feedback

Regardless of the number of students that you are teaching, always be sensitive when giving feedback. Mostly, when you are giving live feedback in front of the camera. Create a balance between your feedback and your students so as not to hurt a student's feelings. Provide proper encouragement when giving feedback.

Make It Actionable

Avoid using vague words when giving feedback. Use feedbacks like "it needs work" or "good job." Explain to the student what he did right and what he did wrong. If the student's work stood out, give him positive feedback with lots of accolades. If there is room for improvement, also let the student know. Point out the areas that need improvement. Let your feedback inspire your students.

Personalize Your Feedback

Your students might be feeling isolated since it is long-distance learning. Personalizing your feedback will give a sense of satisfaction to your student and inspire him to work harder. You can add a student's name when sending feedback. It will help to develop your connection with the student. So, drop your generic feedback and focus on individual feedback.

Use Audio

It might be time-consuming integrating audio feedback. But it is a perfect way of establishing a long-lasting bond between you and your students. Mention the student's name when you want to send audio feedback. It will help to build the student's confidence.

Be Timely

It is imperative if you're going to win the heart of your students. Leaving the students waiting for days before you can give them feedback can affect their moral. It can affect their zeal towards the course.

When you send the student feedback on time, it makes the student feel that you are actively involved and gives him the reassurance that you are fully committed to the course. Always try to reply to each feedback within 24 hours so that the assignment is still fresh in the student's mind.

Encourage Peer Review

That is a situation where you allow students to review each other's works. It helps to promote interaction and engagement between students. Most times, you can sit on your chair and serve as the moderator while your students review each other's work. To make the session more appealing, you can come up with feedback metrics that students can consider while critiquing each other's works.

Using the above feedback strategies will help you to build self-confidence within your students.

No matter the type of work your student submits, always find a way to inspire the student to work harder.

CHAPTER 6:

Fostering Student Persistence and Success

Build Highways for Student Success

You could spend a ton of time perfecting your zoom face-to-face lectures to be delivered online, but do not do this, the payoff isn't really worth it.

You could spend a ton of time recording and editing and rerecording and reediting your lectures to be delivered as videos, but do not do this, the payoff isn't really worth it.

You could spend a ton of time revising your assignments so that students can do them on their own better, but do not do this, the payoff isn't really worth it.

You could spend a ton of time individually emailing and soothing your students so that they feel better, but do not do this, the payoff isn't really worth it.

Instead, spend your limited time available for teaching you building extremely clear "what to do today" pathways for your students to follow that, if they do them, they will nearly be guaranteed success.

Students who are used to face-to-face classes are as bewildered as most of their faculty are when it comes to how to do an online class. If you do nothing else, the absolute best thing you can do is provide a highly structured, due date-oriented, list of tasks for students to follow.

The best way to do this is to include a checklist.

Done By 7 pm Monday	Create a bullet-point outline of the textbook
Done By 7 pm Wednesday	Submit answers to end-of-topic questions
Done By 7 pm Friday	Finish watching this week's online video assignment and have submitted 2 discussion posts

Without going into a monograph's worth of detail, we know about scholarly studies of end-of-course teaching evaluations boils down to this. Students score professors' high if students believe:

1. The professor really wanted them to be successful in learning this material; and
2. The professor built and followed a clear learning pathway that leads to student success.

Kindly note that the phrasing here is quite specific. The phrase is NOT what the professor believes or hopes to be true or intuitively apparent; the phrase is actually focused on what the students perceive about their professor's actions, intentions, and inclination. Your number one pathway to survival is to unambiguously construct an express lane highway with clearly labeled road signs and turn-by-turn directions that students can follow that obvious lead to learning the material and being rewarded with a grade that reflects that learning. If you do anything otherwise, your end-of-course evaluations will suffer mercilessly.

Some faculty manage to get higher than anticipated end of course evaluation scores because they have affable personalities. But a likable personality won't really work in an online course. Online teachers have to motivate through structures and reason rather than personality. Building a clear pathway to success is your key to high marks in this unprecedented time.

Avoid a Correspondence Course

There are two pitfalls to avoid when teaching your online course. The first is not having an abundantly clear pathway for your students to follow that leads to success. The second is making your pathway completely devoid of human contact.

Correspondence courses have been around for nearly a century. In a traditional correspondence course, a student completes a series of readings, submits answers to assigned end of topic questions for a textbook, and perhaps sends in a term paper or two. The reason that this is called a correspondence course is because they traditionally have been relatively self-paced and that assignments were submitted by mail, and graded work was returned to the student by mail. By and large, correspondence courses, all suffered from the same disease—a 90 percent dropout and non-completion rate. This turned out to be true no matter how excellently constructed the course designs were or how high aptitude and self-motivated the students were. Nonetheless, colleges and universities continued delivering these courses for decades upon decades because correspondence courses provided what appeared to be a valuable service and they were fantastic cash revenue generators.

A few decades ago, when faculty first started experimenting with online courses, the default setting was for well-meaning faculty create a correspondence course that looked exactly like the traditional correspondence courses of the past, but assignments were now to be submitted by email (or fax). The problem was that these first-generation online courses suffered from precisely the same ill as the correspondence courses, a giant drop out and non-completion rate.

What faculty focused on improving online teaching figured out was that increasing the student success rate required two specific things that weren't present in conventional correspondence courses. The first is that students needed to feel like they were part of a class, a cohort, or a team. In other words, they needed to feel like their efforts were noticed and that their work mattered. Most faculty accomplish this through required online, asynchronous discussion participation with predetermined discussion questions that are highly relevant to the students. A few postings a week is all that is required. In fact, more than a few required engagements a week quickly turns into thoughtless, perfunctory work and the engagement effect goes away.

The second is that self-pacing didn't work. If you have a largely self-paced course, then students are essentially isolated all over again and have no one to talk to about their assignments because everyone is on a different topic of the book. Instead, course success rates went up when the cohort of students moved together through the course material.

When these two ideas—facilitated and reasonable student-to-student interactions and scheduled pathways for success—were included, all of a sudden, online courses started seeing much higher rates of student success, completion, and, above all, satisfaction with the course. What's even better, is that the faculty enjoyed teaching these courses more often.

Avoid Weekend Due Dates

In the early years of online courses, many of us would set our weekly assignment deadlines for 11:59 pm, Sunday night. The mistaken thinking was that students would benefit from the weekend to get their work done.

What we learned is that students would rush to do their entire weeks' worth of work on Sunday evening, and the quality of work was often lacking. Instead, a simple change seemed to fix everything. We started releasing module assignments starting on Wednesday mornings and have the final assignment component due on Tuesdays at 7 pm. This avoided the weekend deadlines all the other amateur online teachers were assigning—a conflict with which our students greatly appreciated—and kept our students from planning to do their work late into the less productive oil lamp burning hours. Release your highly structured assignment at the same time each week and pick a midweek, early evening due date.

Pathways for Your Success

Unquestionably, teaching online is a lot of work. Online teaching requires you to motivate your students with logic and reason rather than with a gregarious personality. Online teaching requires you to preplan everything as bird-walk, storytime just doesn't happen as it does in a face-to-face class. And, if you're not careful, it can become too much work and keep you for doing the equally valuable, if not more valuable, things your annual performance review requires of you.

How do you keep from working late into the night and letting your online teaching consume your entire weekend? Just like students need structures and checklists, so do you.

Teaching can easily take 20-30, and even 50-hours each week regardless of whether we're talking about a face-to-face course or an online course—teaching is an infinite black hole for time, and there is always something else that could be done. However, for your own health and well-being, successful and productive stay-at-home academics must be ruthless: When your predetermined time allotment has expired, you must stop and say, "Is enough for this week."

Here is how to know if you're off track. If you're answering student emails at 9 pm, you're not doing online teaching right. You need to have a set time frame that you answer student emails, and when that time frame has expired, you do not answer any more student emails. There are no students' emails to which you can answer at 9 pm that make a life-and-death situation workable for a student that couldn't be answered the next afternoon. In fact, I believe that student email queries deserve a seriously thoughtful response with complete sentences and punctuation, rather than a rapid, off-the-cuff response from your cell phone.

The second thing you need is a checklist. Just like your students need a structured pathway for success, so do you. You should write down your SOP (standard operating procedures) for teaching your online class—especially if you get sick and someone needs to take over for you. This should be a written list of what you do and when you do it, so that when you've done it, you can say "I'm sufficiently done," and move on to your next task. What days and at what time do you post the next assignment? What days and at what time do you finalize your design for the next assignment? What days and at what time do you grade student work? What days and what times do you go in and guide any online discussions. What days and at what times do you respond to student emails? Pro-Tip: It is not whenever they arrive in your inbox!

CHAPTER 7:

Creating Autonomy

Learner autonomy can be encouraged in online activities by providing opportunities for learners to control the direction of project outcomes, scaffolding, embedding reflection into classroom activities, and allowing choice in topics. Examples of this include the following:

- Open a social discussion forum and ask students to share their interests and hobbies. Then use this information to personalize learning opportunities.
- Require that students complete learning logs, reflection journals, or checklists to document their own learning.
- Allow learners to make decisions in the creation of an "Our Town" community resource.

Active Participation

Active participation encompasses interactions within the learning community, as well as engagement with the content being studied, and it occurs through such activities as question generation, hypothesis development, and defense of ideas within communities of discourse.

It is important for teachers to establish a nurturing environment, where students feel connected and empowered to participate and take risks. In fact, when online interactions are well structured, it is difficult for students to be passive participants, as there is nowhere to hide. It has also been noted that group members using these types of communication tools participate more equally and produce more independent opinions than students who have only face-to-face group interactions. This phenomenon may be attributed to an increased sense of comfort among students who might be hesitant to participate in face-to-face environments due to status and social context issues

Active participation can be encouraged by providing opportunities for learners to actively engage with the content while developing leadership skills. Here are some examples of this:

- Assign a tech-savvy student to monitor the "Tech Help" class discussion forum.
- While covering a unit on global warming, have students sign up to lead a weekly discussion, either individually or with teammates.
- In a collaborative book-writing project, have students submit applications to be chosen as the project editor.
- Assign the following group leader roles in a collaborative project exploring animal extinction: Lead Research, Lead Author, Lead Explorer, and Lead Geographer.

Collaboration and Community Building

The foundation of effective collaborative efforts stems from feelings of community that has been linked to a sense of well-being, improved cooperation among learners, increased engagement, increased commitment to group goals, increased flow of information, and increased satisfaction in group interactions (Rovai, 2002). Community building through interaction involves a complex array of social, technological, and instructional variables and is key to developing successful social and collaborative connections. Research about the interaction is founded on the concept of transactional distance. Transactional distance refers to the psychological distance experienced by learners in an online community and is affected by both the quality and quantity of interactions within that community (Moore, 1989).

In traditional classrooms, a concerted effort is often needed to establish distance between learners and the instructor for the purpose of maintaining control of the classroom. You will likely find that the opposite is true in online environments. Establishing open lines of communication between you and your students is essential to the learning process and often means that you must lessen the psychological distance between you and them. Synchronous and asynchronous communication tools—such as the telephone, instant messaging, audio and video conferencing, and threaded discussions—facilitate both socially and educationally oriented interactions in online environments.

Community building in any classroom starts from day one. In the online classroom, it is a continuous process and can be encouraged by providing opportunities for learners to engage in social dialogue with their classmates. Suggestions include the following:

- Establish a threaded discussion forum called "Student Lounge" for the specific purpose of social interaction. Establish acceptable use policies and monitor this forum, but allow students to use it freely as a place to socialize with peers.
- Establish a threaded discussion forum called "Think Tank," in which students can pose questions and have them answered by classmates.

Authentic Assessments

Instructional environments that promote a process, rather than an end product, necessitate the development of assessments that are progressive, rather than summative. Although knowledge of standards-based content is an important outcome of learning, measuring the key skills associated with learning processes (i.e., collaboration, communication, problem-solving, and teamwork) and the application of those skills are equally important. To this end, online instructional strategies should encourage the use of a variety of metacognitive activities for assessment, including feedback, self-reflection and self-explanation. Online environments can facilitate content and process evaluation by providing opportunities for data collection and archival. Threaded discussions, recorded audio and video conference sessions, and shared collaborative spaces are just a few examples of tools that provide an opportunity for reflective evaluation of thought processes.

The creation of authentic learning experiences and the authentic assessments that accompany them are highly encouraged in learner-centered environments. The acquisition of knowledge and skills in using Web-based tools by learners makes online environments particularly effective in facilitating the development of assignments and projects that can be disseminated to audiences outside the classroom.

Courses that incorporate authentic assessments provide opportunities for learners to critically reflect on course content and objectives. In addition, they provide opportunities for the public display of learner-created projects, as illustrated by these examples:

- Establish a private space for learners to reflect on project or assignment goals and objectives using a private threaded discussion forum or a Web-based collaborative tool like Google Docs. Google Docs allows the user to invite collaborators to view or edit their work.
- Create a collaborative class project development space such as Google Sites that can be opened to the public. Assign roles to facilitate structure and small group cooperation.

CHAPTER 8:

Making Connections

Effective Communication in Teaching

The "word" communication is very current and broadly recalls the contemporary cultural system: around this discipline have been elaborated models and theories... until its abuse.

Recall that the cognitive activities of our brain have a "mode of operation" for images. It is, therefore, necessary to "stimulate and facilitate" these modes of operation. How? The most effective strategies have to do with the use of a language-centered on metaphors and aphorisms, rhetorical figures widely used in the classical world.

Use apt metaphors and aphorisms, by distributing them in the various phases in which the educational activities are usually broken down, allows you to facilitate learning and to give a real sense of the knowledge-generating in the young students the skill of "meta-reflection," which will enable them to go beyond the reflections of the first level, encouraging the ability of "problem setting," "problem-solving" and "critical thinking instead."

Strategic Communication, centered on the wise use of words, is no longer based on rigid teaching according to a "linear logic" that, very often, clashes with the distraction of young people or with feelings of fatigue and criticality in transmitting skills and knowledge. Indeed, these are not pleasant sensations and excellent dynamics that come to be created in the "class system." On the contrary, they are demeaning and frustrating for teachers but also students.

So, how to build what the great Alfred de Musset (French poet and writer) called the "almost perfect lesson" and many other pedagogues call the "optimal condition" for teaching at school?

Understanding Codes

Technically, codes are sets of signs and rules, shared, that allow the transit of meanings from the issuer to the recipient. In our case, the words of the language English (verbal code), the volume of the voice (shouting "silence!!!" students understand that they must be quiet, but also that we are angry) and the gesture of the raised hand (code not verbal) convey meanings that students clearly understand because shared in our culture.

Knowledge and control of codes allow us to use techniques communications that make effective communication as a function of a good relationship with students. The first step, I repeat, is to know and own a theoretical communication model: this, on the one hand, produces in the senior teacher awareness and, above all, greater professional security; on the other hand, knowing and controlling the factors of communication, and in particular, the codes, allows the teacher to use tried and tested techniques and to invent new ones, also giving vent to their creativity. But I immediately clear the field of possible misunderstandings: the communication techniques they are not magic potions; they often work, but sometimes do not reach the effects are arrows for our bow that enrich our chances of choice and communication.

Communicative Techniques

As I said, the verbal code we use with our students is, most importantly, the English language and its words. Through the verbal code, we communicate the relevant contents of our lesson, but we also establish relationships. Let's see some communicative techniques that we can use by checking the verbal code.

Call the Student by Name

Psychology teaches that feeling called by our name, obviously without exaggeration, makes us feel somewhat more recognized and considered; we are used to hearing it pronounce since we were children, and this contributes to making it able to catalyze our attention in an instant. Address to the student calling him by name during an explanation, "Matthew do you agree?" "Matthew is, do you understand what I said? Did I explain myself?" because he is distracted, or simply because we believe that Matthew should be encouraged, and we want to strengthen the relationship with him-it is a way to make him feel present to us, to recall his whole being. The intention must be positive, voice, and non-verbal messages (which we will then learn about). They must be consistent with our good intentions. This simple communicative technique, as well as having a positive effect on the relationship with the student Matthew (but, during the lesson I will take care to "call" other students too), has a positive impact on attracting attention also on all other students. If Matthew were distracted, we would add to the technique of the name that of the feedback.

Affiliate Humor

Psychologists argue that a comical-humorous attitude within the group, in general, can only establish a climate suitable for the development of curiosity, exploration, attention, and consequently, to prepare to give practical and decisive responses in the learning processes. Not only that. The positive and benevolent wit joke encourages friendships, bonding, emotional stability, psychological and social well-being, higher and significant levels of self-esteem, improves the quality of relationships. In class, the simple joke or comic-humorous story, proposed by the teacher, allows to take a recreational break; it will enable everyone, teacher and students, to unload the possible tensions or, to prepare for a new phase of concentration and school commitment. It is not a question of appearing superficial and frivolous. On the opposing idea:

it is a question of using communicative techniques capable of changing the mood itself within the class. A joke of the teacher can be handy to indicate, with more lightness, mistakes, and wrong behaviors. Thus, the same objection can wear the clothes of hilarity that, a lot, affects much more effectively than a real direct warning.

The Non-Verbal Code

The non-verbal code concerns all the messages that, during the lesson, we send to the students with the eyes, the mimicry, the posture, the gesture, and the proxemics.

We communicate continuously with our body, seamlessly; the non-verbal messages we send with our body are many, including the rhythm and intensity of breathing. But, for what we are interested in, that is, communication in the classroom (online or not), keeping those indicated under control is more than enough. Let's see them one by one.

The Eyes

As we have already said, are essential for establishing and maintaining psychological contact with students.

To look into the student's eyes means to be aware of them, to confirm our interest in them. As we said, we must take turns looking at all the students so that everyone feels that they are being held in equal regard.

The eyes must smile and send positive messages. But we can also use them to blame, to communicate our disagreement for inappropriate behavior. A glance, sometimes, is worth more than many words: in the good and the evil.

The look coherently accompanies the expressions of the face, that is, the mimic.

The Mimic

By this term, all the movements of the face as a whole or its parts. Mimics, therefore, has to do with the use of facial muscles: frowning, smiling, etc., dramatizing the meanings we want to communicate us to be more effective in communication. Remember that the most expressive parts of the face are the mouth and eyes.

The Posture

The posture of the body, the attitude that our body takes in the space of the classroom, which can be rigid or soft, open or closed, with the different gradations in the continuum between the first and second term, communicates our level of nervous tension. Again, we can make our communicative intention more effective by using the nervous tension of the body to achieve our communicative goals. Remember that an upright and toned posture conveys an impression of authority.

The Gestures

The gestures of the hands, united or disjointed, near or far from the body, up or down, open or closed, etc. must emphasize what the words are saying, making them more or less expressive and more easily interpretable.

Hands must harmoniously emphasize speech. It is necessary to speak with your hands: this involves the student and clarifies the content of the speech.

We bend the forearms and keep the hands medium-high and relaxed. Broad gestures give a definite emphasis, showing our enthusiasm and interest in what we are saying.

The Proxemics

The proxemics is the control and the use of the classroom' space and, like the other sub-factors, is significant. We must be careful about our position in the room, avoiding defiled places and favoring the central location over the desks.

For example, approach, without looking at it, the student who during our explanation is talking with his mate, it allows us to reach, generally, two different results: first, keep him quiet. The mere proximity of our body to his desk, his "intimate zone," will induce him to silence; second, we avoid that with a verbal objection, like: "John, please shut up," John responds with "but, I wasn't talking!" and, if John is controversial, the serenity of the lesson can be compromised by the opening of a conflict "You Professor! Are angry with me... Reproaches me without reason...etc." Also, the use of space is useful to recall a general fall of attention. In these cases, you can try to cross the classroom passing between the desks, thus approaching all the students and setting in motion the same mechanism described above. We use space, therefore, to be easily visible to all, to interrupt the perceptual monotony, and to reactivate the attention of the students.

All the sub-factors indicated are tools that we can use for different purposes. We can use them to recall the attention or to make more expressive a concept, a fact, etc. The knowledge of all these factors, therefore, allows us to use the teaching communication strategically. Just that? Yeah, that's it! But, between saying is doing...there is the sea!

The sea, which is at stake. However, is nothing more than knowledge, experimentation and reflection, experimentation and reflection...and so on!

CHAPTER 9:

Developing as an Online Instructor

Daily Practices to Be an Effective Online Teacher

What Do You Need to Learn First?

The first goal of online classes is to attract and engage students, which is still a daunting task for most teachers. The Internet has given us the right tools to simplify our work. Once you have thought about finding the right forum and creating online classes, you need to design your curriculum so that it is focused and committed to your students. It takes a little extra work to find out why students get involved in social media or what they read online. This basic tool helps you connect with students and sometimes these classroom references (with memoranda or examples) help them learn and memorize concepts. Students always respond positively to someone who understands them, so first learn what you like.

Preparation of New Teaching Materials

The Internet offers people easy access to the vast amount of information they expect to be discovered. List the front pages of the course and regularly search for new topics that students may find helpful. When preparing your curriculum, consider the following:

Introduce the audience

Before you start an online course, it is good to know the names of the students.

pag. 66

Plan a week and contact each student to learn about their history and interests. If an appointment is not possible, order online group chats to connect.

This way, you will understand the students during the course and you will need to set learning objectives before preparing a plan for each lesson.

Create Emotional Content for Your Students

Students respond better by explaining concepts with examples that may be emotionally related to each other. Managing these memorable moments makes it easier for them to remember difficult concepts.

Example: Almost all online students attending European football are passionate about football. So, to explain the concept of linguistics, I now include in my notes a serious accident that occurred over the weekend.

Add Nice Graphics

It's almost boring to move back and forth between text slips in the classroom. Here you have to present something funny, like an image .gif, a meme or a short film, a 1-minute harvest, etc. And when students practice questions, they can use a fun timer to set the calculation.

Example: to teach language students, I use a classic Big Bang Theory quote between Leonard and Sheldon in "6 noble gas."

Remember the concepts with cards and games

A license card is a very useful tool to facilitate student attraction and review. In the online environment, there are many features that make traditional maps more useful.

Example: I create Cram cards to add properly played audio clips to each clip, add images, and play integrated memory games for each set of cards I create.

Take an interactive quiz every week

Another purpose of online learning is to get students into exams as they look a little away from their desks. To make this interesting and keep students untouched, you can play a fun quiz while answering questions.

With the help of a weekly quiz, students can always review and direct courses, which is very important for ESL students. By participating in challenging quizzes, learning can be easy and fun for young students.

Top 5 Qualities of Effective Online Teachers

Teaching online does not have to diminish your engagement with your learners. You can create an exceptional online experience through careful planning, preparation, and creating a supportive environment for your students.

You can instruct in an exceptional way by preparing in an exceptional way. You can elevate your online teaching to excellence through planning each phase of the lesson. By creating a supportive environment, you can become the instructor your students admire and relate to.

Always Prepared

Top online instructors are always prepared, which means knowing your subject thoroughly, having all your materials handy, testing your technology, and making yourself ready to perform at your best. Excellent online instructors are not stressed, hurried, or confused.

Prepare for your lessons by taking some time before it to sit quietly and concentrate on what you want to accomplish. Learn to order your thoughts and concentrate, rather than trying to multitask and do a lot of last-minute tasks. You will come across as a focused and prepared online instructor.

Expertise

It's not enough to understand your lesson, as you must also understand your subject. That means you know details and exceptions that may come up when students ask questions, and you are prepared to handle topics that may not be in your lesson plan. In short, exceptional online instructors prepare by mastering the broad subject and not just the narrow topics of the lesson.

Resourceful and Techie

If you believe you might want to use a quote from a book, have that book nearby during your lesson. You may also want to hold up objects. Have all of your materials where you can reach them, as there is nothing more distracting than leaving the camera frame to retrieve an object. Do not let your technology diminish your excellence. Test your computer's software for broadcasting the lesson, even if it worked perfectly the last time you taught. Check keyboard functionality so that you will be able to type. Make sure your microphone is in good working order. Also, use virus-protecting software to rid your computer of any viruses that could slow down the lesson.

Plans Ahead

Exceptional online instructors plan their lessons thoroughly. Begin by asking a question yourself what you want your learners to be able to do at the end of the session. Then build the lesson so that students will understand what you want them to have when the lesson is over. Consider using a storyboard, which is a simple step-by-step sketch of important visuals and the accompanying script. You can imagine each step of the lesson, including what visuals you want to use to enhance topics. Draw examples for each step of the lesson. For example, if you are going to include a graph, draw a rough graph and put notes about what you will say about that graph. You can do this for each major point in your lesson.

The storyboard process enables you to outline your lesson in an orderly manner so that you "scaffold" your instruction. Scaffolding is the art of building a framework from the ground up so that you arrive at the peak of your lesson with firm support. Think in terms of a strong foundation, support in the middle, and a final firm platform at the top.

Plan for the unexpected. If you are going to have a question-and-answer period, plan to use different screenshots, software, or live demonstrations to answer the questions. Have a repertoire of answers you can give to questions, along with the tools to demonstrate those answers.

Your planning should include the timing of the lesson. Practice giving the lesson and using a stopwatch. Limit the lesson to the time allotted, including enough time to answer questions. Excellent online instructors fit the lesson to the time slot and don't have to make excuses for running longer.

Planning means knowing where the lesson leads. Excellent instructors teach lessons that lead to the next lesson. Know what the next lesson will be about, and tell students what that lesson will cover. This will give your online teaching flow and a purpose.

Create a Supportive Environment

You can create a supportive environment through the use of formative assessments: questions, quizzes, and discussions in the middle of the lesson. Pepper your instruction with pauses where you make sure your learners are understanding the points you are making. Make it clear that you are not grading these assessments and that you are using them because you want to support your students' understanding of the lesson.

If you have the ability to communicate in two-way discussions, then initiate an informal chat. Show that you want to take the time to make sure students can ask questions and improve their understanding. If you can't chat, ask pointed questions designed to help learners think about what they've learned. This will show that you are helping students understand and grow instead of just talking to them.

Another way to generate a supportive environment is to offer the students alternate ways to show that they have learned the lesson. Instead of providing a formal test at the end, allow the students to create projects such as visual presentations. Even though you are teaching online, you can ask students to send their presentations to you. Also, offer to listen to verbal presentations. This can be settled through a phone call or by two-way computer communication. These alternative tests can make students feel supported by showing that you are aware that learners don't always express themselves only through writing but also through visual and verbal presentations.

CHAPTER 10:

How to Assess Students

Online learning doesn't stop scheduling classes. You need to assess your students to check out the progress of their learning so far. There is nothing to fear as technology has evolved and included a way for online assessment for students. All of the online platforms I mentioned earlier– Edmodo, Google Classroom, and Microsoft Teams are designed to help you assess your students for every topic they are taught. Remember that your students are more knowledgeable about technology than you think and will cope well with the chosen method assessment. As you use any of the three classroom platforms, you can adopt the following assessment methods.

Utilizing Quiz

Although this is an old method of assessing students, it is still a reliable and strong means of assessing students. It helps you engage them in the process of learning, and it is effective when it is paired with technology. The answers to quiz questions can be in short form, multiple choices, or true/false form. A benefit of the quiz is that it is often short and makes it easy to assess. Also, it makes it easy to assess your students randomly with similar questions, which will make every student's quiz unique.

Fill-In-The-Blank Cloze Activity Method

Another routine you can make use of to help your students provide a short answer is the fill-in-the-blank cloze activity assessment method. This involves the teachers setting questions on the topics taught during your lessons. In the questions, the teacher will create statements and put blank places in place of some terminology discussed in each topic. The students are either left with choosing an option from a broad choice of options or provide the right answer themselves. This quiz often takes the form of questions and the teacher can assess the answers of their students in diverse ways.

Matching Questions

This is also similar to the multiple-choice method. It involves giving students access to a bank of words or phrases that they can choose the right answer from. This form of assessment is done by the teacher providing text or images, while the students will pick an option in column A and identify an option in column B that corresponds with the option in A. It is more than four options, making it a bit demanding. It is an awesome tool for assessing the mind. It works for diagnostic and formative assessments.

Forum Post

Forum post is a good method of assessing your students on any of the online platforms for learning. It involves requesting the students to post new things or react to old posts.

This will help the instructor to measure the level of the student's understanding of the topic under discussion in order to know their areas of interest and know how best to help them. This method involves giving the students a question that involves critical thinking based on the past topics you have learned in the class.

The students will post their answers online to the forum for their peers to give comments.

The teacher then gauges these comments to see how far the students have gone with their reading materials.

Peer Evaluation and Review

Peer evaluation and review give students the opportunity to review the works of their peers anonymously. You can make use of third-party platforms such as Peer Mark to facilitate the distribution and gathering of data with the use of rubrics or assessment questions. The teacher can log in to track how every student is participating in the ongoing activity and can also see the evaluation of the students for one another.

Poll/Quiz Results in Real-Time

This feature is available on all of the online platforms I have mentioned earlier. Teachers can conduct a poll for their students that will make the students provide responses truthfully and without their identity being revealed. As the teacher, you can pair the poll with forum posts or quiz. You can have the students decide on a forum post, and ask them for the reason they gave the responses during the poll. With the help of clickers or other quiz apps, you can set up a poll for your class. Clickers help to generate and show results for students to know the weight of their responses in relation to the other members of their class.

Exit Cards

This is also referred to as minute papers. It is in the form of a question-and-answer style, which students need to complete between 5 and 15 minutes at the end of the class. Exit cards are often used to request students to engage in critical thinking within a short period of time. The teacher may ask a single question, which will require the students to provide a stream of sentences to explain the central idea of the topic explained in the class. Exit cards give the teacher the opportunity to access the students instantly, helping the teacher to gauge the students' levels of understanding of the topic.

Teachers can gather exit cards through emails or the internal messaging system of the platform.

Using Rubrics for Assessment

In the process of assessing your students, you need a rubric, which is a tool that helps to score and describe the expectations of the teacher concerning the performance of the students on the assignment or projects they are given. The rubric reflects the criteria for responding to the assignment or project question given to students. This shows the area of the students' performance that the teacher will grade. It also shows the descriptors, which is the feature that is related to each dimension of the assignment. Lastly, it displays the performance levels using a rating scale that shows the level of the mastery of the students in relation to each criterion. Rubrics help to provide feedback to students on different forms of assignments ranging from projects, papers, or presentations up to group projects and artistic performance. With rubrics, the teacher spends less time to grade the students by referring to the substantive description, which makes long comments irrelevant. Also, the teacher identifies the strengths and weaknesses of his or her class in order to know where to make the necessary adjustments. It ensures grading consistency and helps to reduce the possibility of being uncertain about the grading. Rubrics help both the teacher and the students to achieve their learning goals easily and effectively. Aside from the methods listed above for assessing students online, there are other tools every teacher can rely on to assess their students on their projects. One of these tools is Turnitin.

Utilizing Turnitin

Turnitin is a proofing and plagiarism detection software that is used to scan through the works of students to seek out marched texts. This is often done by comparing the work of the student with a larger database of works published, and materials available on the internet. Assessing students remotely doesn't give full assurance of integrity and reliability. Hence, the teacher needs to utilize a learning tool such a Turnitin to check whether the students meet the requirements for the assignment or not.

Turnitin works well for instructional purposes. It also has a feature for helping teachers to assess the assignment of their students. This is possible with the Turnitin Assignments. Turnitin Assignments provides access to tools such as rubrics, Quick Marks, Turnitin Feedback Studio, and Peer Marks, which are useful for grading students' assignments and projects. It is easier for the instructor to set up his or her assessment criteria for the students, which is always effective.

Assessing your students online can be carried out in three different stages. These stages will help you achieve a whole analysis of your students' learning performances and abilities. Below are the stages.

Pre-assessment: This involves testing your students before the start of your classes to have full knowledge of their level of understanding. The assessment can be geared toward discovering the best learning style of your students. You will get to know those who learn better by visuals or audio. The result gathered will aid you in making the best decision to teach them and achieve the best result.

Formative Assessment: It will come up during the learning period. This is used to know whether the students understand the topics that are being treated or not. The teacher will also get to see the reaction of the students to the materials and instructions that are given in the course. This will help the instructor to know the level of the students before he or she moves to the next topic.

Summative Assessment: This is used to gather knowledge about the response of the students to what they have acquired over a period of time. It often comes up at the end of a course or learning period.

Chapter 11: Critical Skills to Teach the First Weeks of School

Traditionally the first weeks of school have been used to review the previous year's learning, get a baseline measure of students' skills, and dive into the new grade-level curriculum. While it is going to be critical to administering assessments and gauge students' skill levels, I think there are other priorities before diving straight into pure content-based instruction. The prime concern should be on ensuring that students have the skills they will need to be successful when working independently in the classroom or at home. They can learn about the four geographic regions of California later, that's pure content knowledge. First priorities should be the following:

1. Make sure that everyone knows how to use the technology, applications, and websites commonly used in class and in distance learning. Regardless of whichever management system your district supports (Google C-Suite, Canvas, or Microsoft Teams, for example), ensure that you and your students know how to use the fundamental elements and practice using them. Do we know how to post assignments, see when they were turned in, give feedback, and grade them? Do students know how and where to find their assignments and how to turn them in? Spending time in class practicing these things will save you so much time and frustration later.

Find ways to use technology to help with community building and having fun with the practice. I will make suggestions of what a distance learning plan could look like. But even if you are 100% classroom-based, I suggest making at least a few hours' worth of distance plans where students practice clicking on links, going to external websites to read and answer questions, watching videos, and taking formative assessments. If they have questions, it will be so much easier to answer them and show them when they are with you rather than trying to explain via email, phone, or having to screencast a video to show them.

Early primary grade students should also practice using the appropriate technology and apps. Even if they can't create documents, they are digital natives, and they have been interacting with technology long before they started school. Many schools use programs such as Seesaw where younger students can take videos and photos to make a digital portfolio of their work. Have students practice using these tools sooner rather than later, even if it is tempting to wait until they are a little more mature later in the year.

2. Creating a password cheat sheet for each student and making sure they take a copy home.

3. Assigning at least a digital homework assignment so that any issues students have accessing technology and the internet can be discovered before it's a critical issue. Make it something very engaging such as a digital scavenger hunt or digital escape room exercise. Assigning some high-interest projects will help proactively troubleshoot problems as students find out logging in and turning in assignments at home can be different than logging in at school.

4. Teaching students appropriate research skills and how to evaluate the validity of the information they find. Our pupils have grown up in a world where "Google" is a verb. Their default research strategy is simply to pull up a browser and pop in some keywords. Pupils need to be instructed on how to use the internet correctly, how to fact check, how to dig deeper than just citing the first piece of information they find.

In 2019, Stanford University researchers evaluated over 3,400 high school students' ability to judge the credibility of digital information.

Two-thirds of students couldn't differentiate between news stories and ads that were clearly labeled as "sponsored content." The majority of students were also unable to recognize bias. 96% of them didn't consider that the credibility of a climate change website might be influenced by its ties to a fossil fuel company.

So, it's essential to start teaching these skills at an early age. For younger grades, many teachers begin by exposing students to safe search engines such as Kiddle. The standard first research project is usually an animal report, where students can select something of interest. Students are introduced to kid-sized versions of reputable websites such as NatGeoKids.com or WikiKids.com.

These are all good 1st steps, but even younger students need to be taught that not all things they find on the internet are true. When teaching students as early as first grade, I have directed students to a website I own and had them look at the information. Then I would go in, change the information to something outrageous, and insert a picture of someone famous they knew and claim it was me. Then I would have them pull up the website again. They were amazed that I just changed something "on the internet." The website is actually a ".org" which many students feel is more credible. It is a powerful lesson.

I even suggest showing students something like GoDaddy.com where they can see how easy it is to buy a domain name. For fun, they can see if the domain name for their own name is already taken.

Remember the incident that led me to retreat to the supply closet and sob at the beginning of the book? It was shutting down a student who had a question I didn't have time to answer. Here's how I solved that problem. I set up a fun bulletin board in class titled "Curiosity Parking Lot." I attached a stack of papers next to it. If students had a question that they were curious about, they could write it on a note and attach it to the bulletin board. Whenever we had a few extra minutes, I would grab one, and students would research the answer.

This solved two problems. First, students felt they could get their questions answered, and I was able to model research skills appropriately. Taking a question out of the parking lot became a preferred "may do" activity for early finishers.

Mid-grade and older students definitely should be taught to be discerning about digital research. commonsense.org points out.

"Most of all, it's up to us to show students how to be skeptical of what they see on the web without becoming cynical."

Older students should be taught how to use fact-checking sites and engage in lessons where they evaluate web sources for bias. One of the best materials I have ever found on teaching students how to correctly "google" and truly understand points of view and primary sources is the 2016 TED Talk by Alan November, what is the Value of a Teacher?

In the talk November, a prominent educational consultant, contends teachers overestimate how much critical thinking students use when searching for information. If you are unfamiliar with the talk, I highly recommend listening to his account of working with a student who wrote a report on the Iranian Hostage Crisis.

Ask yourself if your students would do anything other than what this student did, which was type in "Iranian Hostage Crisis" into google and go with the information presented, which is all from the Western perspective. Would you know how to teach a student how to effectively research the issue from the Iranian perspective and apply critical thinking to the problem?

If I taught upper grades, I would definitely watch the appropriate section TED Talk with my students and see how far they could get with the assignment. The whole talk is only 18 minutes. If you're not reading this on a digital reader with the link, just google "Alan November TED Talk, 2016." That part isn't tricky!

Also, for older students, teach them how to "show their work" for web searches with a simple graphic organizer. Media literacy skills are only going to increase in importance moving forward, and they need to be explicitly taught.

5. Discussing the responsibility and best practices of digital citizenship.

Most schools invest time in citizenship, character, and anti-bullying education of one type or another. Digital citizenship is a whole other issue. It is important to spend time at the beginning of the year setting expectations for both internet safety (password and privacy protection, phishing emails, pop-ups that can cause viruses, etc.) and internet etiquette.

Cyberbullying is a big problem. It happens outside of the classroom, with even younger students having their own phones and iPads. The issue is further complicated when the school issues the device and requires it to be used off-campus in the case of distance learning.

While every district has a technology policy that students and parents must sign, we all know how stressful it is to be perceived as responsible for managing things over which we have no control. Here's an example. During shelter in place, my third-grade students had their own "google hangouts" and sent messages to each other. They did this on their own, outside of any requirements I had for collaboration.

Clearly, I have no control over what they choose to do on their own time in their own home, even if it is on a device the school provided. One morning, I received an email from a parent saying that his child hadn't slept all night and was extremely scared because another student had sent her a chain letter in an email.

I remember chain letters from my childhood when, old school style, we got them in the mail. They usually contain a scary story and a threat of a curse if you don't forward it to ten other people—that kind of thing.

The parent sent me the email. Let's just say it was graphically violent and disturbing. I spent the whole day playing detective, trying to figure out who had sent it to who, calling parents and students, and my IT department.

Students were scared first by the content, and then some of them were afraid of telling their parents because they had lied and said they were doing required school work when they were on hangouts with their friends. I emailed all parents and reminded them that if students make their own chat rooms, there is no supervision provided by the school. In addition, I had specific Zoom calls with the entire class about the issue. The IT department confirmed that the letter did not originate in my class.

Nonetheless, parents' perception was that it was something I needed to resolve and manage. Don't get me wrong; they were my students, and they were scared, so I felt absolutely motivated to help. But are these things a teacher's responsibility? The lines are very gray here. Time, energy, and resources were wasted. Worse, students were scared and stressed. In extreme cases, cyberbullying is a factor in teen suicides.

It is easier to see how the teacher can influence this when we have students with us six hours a day; it's less obvious when working with them remotely. The answer is to invest time upfront in digital citizenship lessons. If your school has not already adopted resources for this, I urge you to invest adequate time in finding your own. I understand there are so many things to cover at the beginning of the year and it's tempting to rush through these lessons. But having students role-play and really understand the power of their words is such an important skill. Everyone is becoming increasingly reliant on sound bites, tweets, quick texts, and emojis to communicate. Students who have grown up spending a lot of time chatting via a screen need to be explicitly taught that feelings are real, not just graphics.

CHAPTER 12:

Ways to End a Lesson and Expectations

As an instructor, you have the opportunity to say some concluding words, and in those hurried moments, create a sense of closure. For both the professor and the students, the end of the online semester can be anticlimactic. It lacks that sense of closure we have grown to expect. As well, in our weariness, it's easy to become erratic and hurried in our communication.

Here Are 5 Creative Ideas for Successfully Bringing Your Lesson to a Close

1. Takeaway Discussions

Create an optional discussion forum as a place for students to share their takeaways from the lesson. This is an excellent way to integrate reflective learning into the course while bringing a sense of closure. Better yet, make this a required and integral element in your course design. Within your discussion prompt, ask students to share how the course has impacted their personal and professional lives. If you work with high school students, ask them to reflect on the "highlights of the course" or what impacted them the most.

2. Employ Culminating Assignments

Culminating assignments can bring a sense of closure to the lessons and are excellent ways to assess your student's learning. Some examples of culminating assignments are portfolios, integrative papers, panel presentations, reflection on real-life experience, timelines, and mini-projects. Culminating activities can become cumbersome, so consider scaling them down for your students. The power in these assignments is that they tend to move your students into higher-order thinking skills, and contain both reflective and integrative components. Because these require a significant amount of planning and scaffolding, these should be explained and developed early in the course.

3. Concluding Email

Send out a concluding email with your own takeaways from the lesson. Perhaps you've read a new book that you would like to recommend for further study. You might offer some concluding thoughts on how your students might integrate the subject matter into their own professional development. If you are working with secondary students, explain how the course might benefit them in their future courses and life experience. Share from your own story, and share what you have enjoyed about your students.

4. Host a Q&A Web Conference

This is more technical and takes more prep work, but it can be incredibly effective. Because the last weeks of the quarter or semester are so hectic, I recommend situating your web conference in the third week from the end of the course. Here is one proven format: First, ask (or require) your students to email you questions that they have had during the course. This gives you material to prepare. Second, invite your students to attend the live conference, letting them know that they will be able to share additional questions via live audio or chat. You may want to prepare a few brief slides to share during the web conference in order to add a visual element.

It's important to remember that students take online courses because they are flexible and largely asynchronous. This means that web-conferences are best kept optional. If they are required as part of the course, offer several opportunities for your students to connect. If your learners are adults, this will mean after work hours. Another solution is to record the webinar and make it available to your students after the live session.

5. Plan for It

Now we are back to the idea of leveraging the power of habits and structures. Look over the last weeks of your course. Does its tail off? Or are there elements already built in that require you to interact with your students? If not, consider how you might boost your communication during these weeks. Keep consistent with your weekly emails, and model the kind of engagement you expect from your students.

Parental Expectations

Expectations of parents from an online teacher can vary. Just like with a public-school job as an educator, you will have parents that expect you to go above and far away for their child and some that care less. With online classes, most parents that I have met in the classroom or have left me feedback have been very involved with the learning of their children. Keep in mind that most parents have to pay for the online English-speaking classes, so they do not want to throw away their money on a teacher that is not meeting their expectations for their child or for them as the parent.

1 **Your professional appearance.** You should always open your camera with a professional look. Just because you do not have to leave your house does not mean you should keep your pajamas on. When a student opens their computer in time for class with you, they should see a professional-looking teacher. You should have your hair nicely done or pulled back so the student is able to see your face. Even if you are only seeing children in front of the screen, do not think that the parent is not watching from the side or watching the playback of the class. These parents want their child to have the experience of their child

feeling like they are in an actual classroom. So, in your background while on your computer, make sure you do not have clutter or clothes thrown around. Your surrounding will greatly affect the way you appear as a professional educator. Most companies ask that you look professional by wearing a certain color. The color is usually a symbol that the parents are able to associate with the teacher working for the company. It is always nice to dress up whatever you are wearing by having a simple blazer to put over your shirt. You could even go as far as wearing a very nice necklace to dress up your attire. For women, makeup is a big plus. Makeup can make the skin glow and you appear very bright and fresh while teaching class. Don't forget that lipstick! A nice bold lipstick (not neon colors) will help your lips to pop out for the student. When talking the student will often pay close attention to your lips. Overall, parents are looking for a nice clean look from you as the professional. No one wants their teacher to look like they don't care or just rolled out of bed.

2   **Your professional attitude.** Your professional attitude means a lot to parents no matter what company you work for. You should always come to class with a bright smile and ready to teach. Come to class being ready to teach and excited to see your student. Perhaps you did not want to see a certain student today because of their last classroom behavior, but just remember that the class will only last for a short period of time. That alone should be enough to make you smile. Just set to the side, feelings you may have about a student for whatever the reasons may be and have them enjoy learning the lesson. Your professional attitude she always remains positive with full of smiles.

CHAPTER 13:

How to Motivate Pupils

Inspiration, truth be told, is one of the principal establishments of a compelling classroom. As an educator, you will never at any point arrive at the objective without rousing your understudies. Inspiration really is certifiably not a convoluted term and it is additionally not a troublesome undertaking to propel your understudies. We are experiencing our lives with satisfaction and bliss, and torment and distresses because we are roused to push ahead. Truly, once in a while in our lives being dismissed and debilitated, we stop our desire to proceed onward, yet as human instinct, being roused, we again begin to think to proceed onward. So also, in the vast majority of the cases without being spurred, an understudy loses would like to consider. That is the explanation the understudies need inspiration.

An educator can't be a fruitful instructor except if she/he realizes how to persuade an understudy. A fruitful instructor is an individual who knows about the realities and strategies on how she/he can make a successful classroom, where the understudy will partake eagerly. Actually, without rousing your understudy, you won't have the option to satisfy your sole responsibility.

There are numerous approaches to rouse understudies in the Classroom. As an educator with my 12+ long periods of showing encounters, I like to share probably the best tips to spur your understudies in the Classroom.

Actually, such tips on inspiring your understudies will assist you in making your Classroom powerful and creative.

1. Guarantee Fear Free Classroom

Guess what? Dread consistently bars learning results. Along these lines, never at any point attempt to force dread by forcing disciplines in your Classroom. I have seen that a few of us, the educators force additional assignments as a discipline since physical disciplines don't exist in showing these days like the old and traditional period. Besides, demoralizing remarks also acquire dread among the understudies in the Classroom. The dread in the Classroom, be it for discipline or debilitating remarks will never persuade your understudies. Truth be told, dread goes about as a boundary to taking an interest in the learning meeting adequately. The understudy will never attempt to be included effectively in the Classroom. That is the reason each instructor ought to guarantee a dread free classroom to inspire your understudies. In this way, never at any point practice of disheartening remarks and heap of assignments as disciplines.

2. Empower Their Thoughts and Choices

Continuously empower new considerations in the Classroom. While giving assignments and course works, give them their own opportunity to pick the point without anyone else. Your understudies will be spurred.

All things considered; you definitely realize that people like appreciation.

Truth be told, gratefulness changes numerous existences of the understudies. Your understudies will excitedly wait to take part in your next class.

In any event, when you acknowledge new contemplations, many great ideas will likewise be uncovered by different understudies in your Classroom. So constantly welcome new contemplations to persuade your understudies.

3. Explain the Objective

Each understudy clearly prefers clear guidelines. Toward the start of the course, explain every goal and target objective to be accomplished. Remember to examine the impediments they may look during the course. Examine plausible cures of the obstructions they may confront. In this way, they will be spurred to talk about further issues, which will make the subject simple. Consequently, you will find that your Classroom gets powerful since your understudies are inspired.

4. Improve the Classroom Environment

Don't generally sit on your seat to talk about the exercise. Stroll alongside the understudies while talking about the exercise. At times remove them from your Classroom. Take them to the library some of the time to investigate work. The difference in the classroom condition triggers the curiosity of the cerebrum of the students, which is truth be told, a prerequisite of inspiration.

5. Be a Great Listener

Listen cautiously to what your understudy needs to communicate. Value their feels and musings. Find a way to sift through the challenges they are griping about. Be an incredible audience. They will begin preferring you as you hear them out with appropriate consideration. Hence, you can procure their trust. Presently, isn't it simple to persuade them? On the occasion that you need your understudies ought to hear you out, you should hear them out first.

6. Offer Their Experience

Not all understudies will share their experiences during the exercise. Some will be occupied with books. Be that as it may, when a few understudies will examine their experience identified with the exercise, others will be propelled to take part effectively. Set up your exercise so that various sorts of students will take an interest energetically in experience sharing exercise. In such a case, different understudies additionally get persuaded to take part in sharing their own encounters. In this way, you can guarantee a successful classroom.

7. Positive Competition

Competition is, truth be told, a positive system in a classroom. Guarantee positive competition. Positive competition in bunch work spurs students hugely. Indeed, even they are set up to deal with bunch work, which will acquire an extraordinary benefit from their expert life too. It is no denying actuality that positive competition triggers inspiration among your understudies in the Classroom.

8. Realize Your Student Well

You should realize your understudies well. You ought to likewise know their preferences, abhorrence, effectiveness, and lacking. At the point when your understudies comprehend that you realize them well, they will begin loving you and uncovering their obstructions. Then, this will be simpler for you to persuade your understudies on the correct way. Except if realizing them well, you probably won't have the option to spur them.

9. Trust Them and Give Them Responsibility

Give your understudies responsibility. Relegate them some classroom activity. They will include with devotion without a doubt. At the point when you will give them responsibilities, a trust within themselves will develop and they will begin accepting that they are significant since they are getting an incentive from you. Hence, they will be persuaded to partake effectively in the Classroom. At the point when you are confiding in them, consequently, they will confide in you too.

10. Express Your Excitement

Express your excitement in the Classroom during an exercise while they are satisfying their responsibilities. Offer your excitement on their incredible execution. Again, express your positive excitement additionally when another thought is presented by any student. Your appearance of excitement will trigger inspiration for them.

11. Keep Record

Set up a record for you. Write down every one of your understudy's exhibition. At the point when you locate that a specific understudy is improving, talk about the understudy on the improvement. Demonstrate the record to the understudy. Reward and value the understudy before the Classroom. Indeed, even offer the upgrades with the guardians. At the point when an understudy finds that you care for that understudy as you are talking about from your record, the understudy gets propelled.

12. Positive Feedback

At the point when an understudy isn't progressing nicely, give positive criticism. Give additional opportunity if conceivable. Resemble a companion and attempt to comprehend the instance of such a terrible showing. Support the understudy persuading that next time s/he can without much of a stretch improve as s/he was unable to see how to perform well right now the correct information and method. Guess what? Your positive input can change numerous lives. Cautiously take a gander at the most fragile understudies in your Classroom, you will clearly get numerous positive qualities. Illuminate them about such extraordinary qualities they are having. Truth be told, value them, which consequently will propel them essentially.

13. Genuine Situation in the Classroom

Relate your exercise plan with a genuine situation. Make the exercise fascinating with fun and game. Disclose to them a pertinent story with a blend of amusingness. Therefore, the exercise turns out to be simple for the understudy to identify with their own understanding. Let them relate the exercise with their own experience too. Simply monitor fittingly. Truth be told, while you are managing your exercise, all things considered, situations, the understudies become persuaded to learn and go to your group.

Conclusion

You would be surprised at just how many educators are not aware of what Zoom, Canvas, and smartphone applications such as iMovie are capable of. Take time to become familiar with the technology you are using so you can not only improve your methods, but you can really connect with your students and get them excited about online learning.

While virtual learning may feel forced, students will benefit long-term from the transferable skills of self-driven learning. In the future, you may find you are teaching a mix of physical and virtual students. You need to prepare for the new norm of blended learning.

Make sure that you allocate time for one-on-one with your online students. Not every kid likes to ask questions in front of a group. Offer students the ability to meet with you privately to make sure they are progressing. Identify roadblocks and help students work through them.

Tailor activities for virtual and at-home learning. As you know, not everything you do in the classroom can be done at home, so ensuring that every student can gain something from an activity is vital for that balance. Promote growth and learning by pushing students out of their comfort zones and support risk-taking.

Technology advancements and tools are a great way to engage, connect, and help students thrive on their own time. This is especially true since the start of the 2020 pandemic that resulted in millions of students having to rely on virtual learning. Sure, there are some negative sides, as there are with anything, but when implemented properly, the benefits of technology can far outweigh the negatives. Though there are still fundamental learning methods, such as natural handwriting that should not get lost in the digital world, knowing how to give students the best tools to reach their full potential in the classroom (physical and virtual) is the goal.

Education is now changing at an unprecedented speed. Gone are the days when generations of students could relate to 10-year-old books, because the information in them was still relevant. Educators today are being asked to reinvent their teaching styles and reimagine learning. When the world changes this quickly, education methods need to be adapted to fit the learning styles of the day. On top of that, teachers need to learn how to use the technology their school districts have introduced.

It's safe to say that change will be a constant in education. Ironically, teachers are adapting to all of this change and turning their presence into a constant for students. It is my hope that the seismic shifts underway in education and technology will find an equilibrium between people and purpose. Educators will, of course, be required to evolve and change, perhaps faster than they might like. Foundational principles regarding the way we teach, the stories we call, the delivery methods that we use will fall into place. Your first online videos will look silly in one year, but that's okay. Open yourself up to personal growth and your teaching style will adapt. Students will provide the anecdotes you use to adapt and grow.

You have just about finished this book, and I would like to congratulate you. The time you have set aside for professional development should serve you well. Yes, you will need to spend time creating online lessons, video content, mentoring students, and reviewing assignments. But, make time in your schedule to work on your production capabilities.

Keep up the good work, and make time to improve your skills on a continuous basis. Feel free to send me an email. I would love to hear from you.

GOOGLE CLASSROOM FOR TEACHERS STEP BY STEP GUIDE

A BEGINNER'S GUIDE TO GOOGLE CLASSROOM 2020 - 2021. SCREENSHOTS, TIPS, AND TRICKS FOR THE BEST MODERN TEACHER. INCLUDING PILLS OF MINDSET

RICHARD V. ROSS

Introduction

What Is Google Classroom?

Google Classroom is free of charge web service made by Google for schools. It clarifies paperless structure, dissemination, and marking of homework. Google Classroom's underlying goal is to streamline the file-sharing process between teachers and students. Google Classroom incorporates Google Drive for the production and delivery of tasks, Google Docs, Sheets and Slides for writing, Gmail for collaboration, and Google Calendar for scheduling.

Students can be invited via a special code to enter a college, or imported automatically from a school domain. Every class creates a separate folder in the Drive of the respective individual, where the student can send work for a teacher to assess. IOS applications, which are available for IOS and Android devices, allow users to take images and add to assignments, share files from other phones, and offline access. Teachers can track each student's progress and teachers can return work along with the feedback after grading.

But what distinguishes Google Classroom from the standard Google Drive experience is the interface between teacher and student, developed by Google for the way teachers, and students think and work.

Evolution of Google Classroom

Google Classroom was revealed on 6 May 2014 with a preview available to individual members of Google's G Suite for Education program. It was launched publicly on 12 August 2014. By October 2015, Google reported that certain 10 million students and teachers were using it.

Google said about 50 million students and teachers worldwide used Google software from Gmail to Chrome.

In 2015, Google introduced a Classroom API and a website sharing button allowing school administrators and developers to continue their interaction with Google Classroom. In 2015, Google also incorporated Google Calendar into the Classroom for planned assignment dates, field trips, and class speakers.

In 2017, Google enabled Classroom to allow any personal Google users to enter classes without the need for having G Suite or Education account. And, it became possible for any individual Google student to build and teach a course in April of the same year.

In 2018, Google announced a refresh classroom, introducing a classroom section, enhancing the grading interface, allowing teachers to reuse classroom work from other classes, and adding features to organize content by topic. In 2019, Google released 78 new illustrations of the classroom.

For the previous two years, Google has been taking its popular apps and equipping them for classroom use. Although many schools and districts tend to use traditional learning management systems, such as Blackboard, Canvas, Moodle, and Schoology; the eyes of teachers are gradually focusing on Google's Classroom Platform. Most schools are also using the collaboration software suite of Google—Docs, Sheets, and Slides. What Classroom seeks to offer is a way of bringing together these applications and applying new functionality to what teachers and students need. In short, the Classroom is aiming to be a lightweight framework for learning management.

According to the product manager at Google; they spent about a year and a half studying and talking to educators about the app. Apps alert from the guardians and the introduction of multiple teachers to a class were created merely from user feedback.

Does Google Classroom Become An LMS?

Technically, it doesn't. Google Classroom is not a stand-alone program for learning management (LMS), course management (CMS), or student information (SIS) program. That said, Google adds new functions to Google Classroom periodically. For example, in June 2019, Google announced that schools would soon be in a position to synchronize the new grading features of the tool with an existing student information system. As Google continues to add features; it is likely to start looking, becoming more like an LMS to work. Perhaps it's better, for now, to think of the device as a one-stop-shop for class organizing.

Is Google Classroom Free of Cost?

The Google for Education platform is free for schools. Still, there is a paid G Platform Enterprise tier for education, which includes additional features such as advanced video conferencing apps, advanced security, and premium support. Google no longer publishes information about pricing, so you'll want to contact them directly for a quote.

Google also offers several free items for authoring tools, web themes, and professional growth, such as Chromebooks, and partners with other companies.

Implementation and integration

Google provides educators and IT Administrators with a range of training choices. These are:

- The Teacher Hub, which provides primary or advanced self-paced Google Classroom preparation and instructor professional development resources.

- Train the Trainer course for people into teaching others.

- Google software Certified Educator and Certified Instructor programs.

- G Suite Certified Administrator program for IT administrators.

Who Is Eligible for Google Classrooms?

The classroom is open to:

- Schools that use G Suite for Education.

- Organizations that use G Suite for non-profits.

- Individuals over the age of 13 with personal Google accounts. Age can vary according to region.

- Both Domains in the G Suite.

Google Classrooms Support Service

Users can access Google Classroom help in the following ways:

- The Help Centre offers information on different topics related to Google Classroom. There is also a troubleshooting section with solutions to common issues.

- There is a software community where users can seek advice from other Google Classroom users and Google Classroom staff.

- Google Classroom also offers regular updates with new features and other software enhancements.

- IT guides for schools' IT administrators also exist.

Can the Classroom be used if G Suite for Education domain includes Gmail disabled?

Yes. Gmail doesn't have to be enabled to utilize the Classroom. If your administrator has not activated Gmail, however, teachers and students do not receive e-mail notifications.

Note: If you set up your mail server and receive information from Drive, you can receive notifications from the Classroom too.

Could the Classroom be used if G Suite for Education domain has been disabled?

No. Classroom collaborates with Drive, Docs, and other tools offered by G Suite for Education to help teachers build and collect assignments, and students submit work online. If you disable Drive: Docs and other services are also disabled.

You are not able to add these resources to the research that you allocate to students. Students would also not be able to add these to their jobs. The classroom can still be used, but the collection of features is minimal.

Difference between Google Classroom and Google Assignment

Google Assignments is for organizations using a learning management system (LMS) that want better grading workflows and assignments.

It can be utilized as a stand-alone tool and a complement to the LMS, or it can be implemented into the LMS as an interoperability learning tool (LTI) by the school admin.

If you are using the Classroom, you already enjoy the best of tasks, including reports on originality.

Accessing Google Classroom from school account and personal account

Most of the time, the classroom is the same for all users. However, since users of school accounts have access to G Suite for Education, they get further attributes, such as email summaries of student work for guardians and full user account management. G Suite for charity users has the same features as users of G Suite for Education.

Google Classroom for visually impaired people

Google Classroom is a resource designed to help teachers and students interact in the paperless classroom and remain organized there. Visual disability and blindness students can use a screen-reader to access and handle classes and assignments.

Following is the availability for various screen readers:

- **Web:** With any modern browser such as Chrome, Mozilla Firefox, Microsoft, Internet Explorer, or Apple Safari, you may navigate the Classroom using a screen-reader. See the guide on how to set it up in your browser. You can use ChromeVox, for example, with your Chromebook. On Macs, the built-in screen reader, VoiceOver, is used.

- **Mobile:**
    - **Android:** The smartphone app for the Classroom works with TalkBack, a pre-installed screen reader that uses spoken input for interaction.
    - **IOS:** The Virtual Classroom app operates on IOS with VoiceOver. For specifics, you might need to see your device's accessibility settings.

Google Classroom API outline

The Classroom API can be used by schools and technology companies to create applications that communicate with Classroom and G Suite for Education and to make Classroom function better to suit their needs. The Classroom API is an API created by Google. That means non-Google companies will benefit from the resources and infrastructure that Google provides.

To use the Classroom API, developers must adhere to the Terms of Service of the Classroom API. Many programs cannot use Classroom data for marketing purposes. Third-party developers and administrators may use the Classroom API. Teachers and students must approve third-party apps. Utilizing the Classroom API, you can do many of the things that teachers and students can do programmatically through the Classroom UI. For example, you can synchronize with the student information systems, display all the classes taught in an area, and control the coursework.

Non-Google services can use the Classroom API to incorporate Classroom features. For example, an app may allow a teacher to copy and reuse a Google Classroom class, rather than re-create the level and re-add every student. Applications may also display, build, and change Classroom work programmatically, add materials to work, turn students' work in, and return grades to the Classroom.

The software must request authorization from the Classroom user before software or service can access Classroom data. The app asks for the individual permissions it requires (such as a username, email address, or photo profile), and the user may approve or reject the request made by the service. The Classroom API uses a popular Internet standard named OAuth to authorize access.

As an administrator of the G Suite for Education, you monitor how the data is exchanged within a domain. You can decide which teachers and students in your area can allow services to access their Classroom data in the Google Admin Console. By organizational unit; you can customize the access. You can also monitor the services that have been given access to a user's account in your jurisdiction in the Admin console, and you may revoke permissions if required. The different tasks that the Classroom API can accomplish depend on what position a user has in a class. A user can be a student, instructor, or administrator just as in the Classroom UI. Teachers and students should accept applications from third parties and report misconduct.

When the consumer is a (n):

- **Student:** The API can view the course information and teachers for that course.

- **Teacher:** The API can build, display, or remove their classes, show, attach, or remove students and additional teachers from their classes, as well as view and return research, build assignments and topics, and set grades in their classes.

- **Administrator:** The Classroom API can organize, view, or delete any class in their G Suite for Education domain. It can attach or delete students and teachers in their area in all the classes. It also looks at the work and topics in all of the classes in their domain.

There are many explanations for why Google Classrooms are being used for more and more classrooms. The technology is being implemented all around the world, including the US schools and districts through the 1:1 laptop initiative. The initiative features a learning laptop for every pupil. Chromebooks are often chosen because of their affordability and intuitive interface. They are easily integrated with the complete suite of Google apps that includes the Classroom.

CHAPTER 1:

The Modern Teacher

With many online assets, the era can assist improve coaching. Teachers can make use of one-of-a-kind applications or confided in online belongings to develop the customary strategies for coaching and to hold understudies more and more locked in. Virtual exercise plans, comparing programming, and on-line appraisals can help instructors with sparing an exceptional deal time. This sizeable time can be applied for operating with understudies who're fighting. Also, having virtual mastering situations in faculties improves cooperation and statistics sharing between instructors.

Run a Virtual Field Trip

If a place is a long way off due to calculated issues, you may mimic a digital outing by shopping a Google Cardboard for under $15.

There are applications you could use to investigate popular structures, for example, the Empire State Building, and ordinary wonders, for example, the Great Barrier Reef.

You may additionally ask: "By what approach will this interface with gaining knowledge of objective?" You could go to an out of doors milestone, preserving a fake dialogue in that nation's language, or view the region itself from a geographic point of view.

This manner can consist of any other, drawing in factor on your sporting activities.

pag. 108

Review Field Trips Virtually

Likewise, you could utilize Google Earth to investigate areas before clearly traveling them.

Suppose your class is about to visit the Zoo. Discover the area, going through it using Street View to look, which displays provoke the maximum understudy curiosity.

You can swiftly have a look at what they're anticipating, boosting fervor tiers for the excursion.

Mainstream area trip goals will likewise have web sites loaded up with visual media you can use to supplement the review.

Everything vital is a gadget related to a projector or full-size display screen.

Calm a Noisy Classroom

To make it less challenging to present sporting activities and introductions, make use of a device that tracks, and indicates school room clamor.

For instance, Too Noisy is an exact commotion meter. You'll probably locate that—without letting students know—understudies will emerge as tranquil while the meter spikes.

This way implies a massive portion of them won't be as troublesome while you give an exercise or run a loose work action.

They may also even shush one another.

Like this, you'll have a less difficult time introducing content material.

Use Videos for Mini-Lessons

You can guide your exercise designs employing making use of recordings as independent evaluations for specific subjects.

Additionally, reachable as aptitude audits and critiques, numerous web sites have instructor-made video content material. TeacherTube is a case of education just shape of YouTube, protecting center college subjects.

You can scan for a specific topic or peruse by way of class, unexpectedly finding popular recordings. For instance, scanning for "center school variable based totally math" will stack a results web page containing study publications, particular exercises, and test surveys.

This simple approach to utilize technology in the classroom provides a sight and sound component for your sporting events, which could adequately reverberate with visible rookies.

Research has indicated that the usage of enlivened recordings can decidedly affect a youngster's advancement in a few fitness regions such as memory, imagination, primary reasoning, and important thinking.

Co-Ordinate Live Video

You don't want to confine yourself to pre-recorded recordings, as conferencing technology can permit topic experts to convey physical activities.

Regardless of whether it's a contact from some other school or a prepared trainer you connect to, bringing a consultant into your classroom will open your understudies to new thoughts and can help your remaining challenge at hand.

You can include the man or woman as touch on Skype or Google Hangouts; conveying the exercising through this system. Skype even has a rundown of tourist speakers who will intentionally talk approximately their topics of aptitude.

Pose your understudies to devise inquiries, helping them appreciate—and fulling takes a hobby in—this cutting area tackles traditional physical games.

Play Podcasts

Playing massive virtual recordings can beautify your physical games, yet connect with sound-associated newcomers and go about as a learning station.

Made with the aid of bunches extending from media mammoths to traditional individuals active approximately a particular subject; you can find out digital broadcasts which are:

- Meetings with the writer of an e-book your understudies are perusing
- Exercises approximately examining techniques and techniques
- Investigations of an academic plan related subject
- Talks from educators

For a secondary school direction, you might need to shape a mission that allows understudies to make and play their webcasts.

This way is possibly the most effortless approach to utilize technology in your study room—you certainly need a device with a stable audio system.

Add Multimedia Elements to Presentations

Though slideshow introductions made up of content material can withdraw understudies, ones with sight and sound additives can correctly hold their attention by fluctuating substance conveyance.

When relevant, try to include:

- Pictures

- Charts

- Pictographs

- Digital recording cuts

- Audio cues

- Short video exercises

- News, film and TV application cuts

You don't need to search the Internet to find out large charts and pictographs—you can make them yourself. There are loose on-line devices that find a manner to enter information, other marks, and adjust your plan.

Almost certainly, slideshow introductions as of now have an impact on your sporting events, and such as unique sorts of media can make them all the extra charming.

Send Adaptive Content

If each considered one of your understudies has a mobile telephone and is always on it, why now not utilize the circumstance to, in addition, your potential advantage with the aid of conveying content material through the telephones?

There are versatile getting to know packages that understudies can access through tablets and cell phones.

For instance, ClassK12 offers sentence structure exercises as much as sixth grade Common Core gauges. It's produced from versatile programs that understudies can download onto their gadgets. As a teacher, you may make virtual classrooms, carry assignments, and run reports.

Conveying appropriate substances through such projects may also appear difficult, yet the procedure is typically natural and robotized.

Offer an Online Class Calendar

To hold understudies knowledgeable concerning the substance, they'll be coping with, make, and offer a class schedule that subtleties exercises and capabilities large dates.

You can utilize software, for example, Google Calendar, messaging your schedule's hyperlink on your understudies or their folks.

This manner maintains them educated, yet causes you to continue to be sorted out—you'll rapidly check whether or not you've set an excessive wide variety of due dates in a quick period. Furthermore, by retaining understudies on the up and up; you'll help them with coming arranged for every class.

CHAPTER 2:

Pills of Mindset

Google Classroom was built for both the educator and the learner in mind. It isn't only the teachers who can do so many things with Google Classroom, but students can also harness the full capabilities of this application. The student's reaction to Google Classroom is whenever the teacher, who is the main Manager of the Classroom, uploads content in the Classroom.

Here are some of the various things that students can do with Google Classroom:

- **Change Ownership:** When you turn in an assignment, the teacher becomes the owner of your document. You are no longer the owner, and therefore you are unable to edit the text. Turned in the wrong assignment? Simply click on the 'Unsubmitted' button. You would need to refresh Google Classroom once you un-submit so that you can resend a new document.

- **Assignment listings:** Students can find a list of all the assignments created by teachers by clicking on the menu icon located at the top left-hand corner of Google Classroom. Practically all assignments that have not been archived can be viewed in this list.

- **Utilize the Mobile App for easier access:** We know students are always on their mobile phones. One of the best ways to get notified if you have a new assignment is through the Google

Classroom's mobile app. The mobile app can be downloaded and installed from the Playstore or iTunes. The app allows students to view their assignments and submit their work directly from the app. This mainly works when students are requested to submit real-life samples, or a video or a combination of photos. All they need to do is take pictures of their samples or their solutions and then upload it to the Google Classroom.

- **No worries if you haven't clicked on save:** Encourage your students to use Google Docs to do their assignments. If you have given work that requires them to write reports, write a story, or anything that requires their use of a Word document, use Google Docs because it saves edits automatically. This eliminates your student's excuses for not being able to complete their homework because they did not save it. Also, it just makes things easier when you are so engrossed with completing your work, you forget to save; Google Docs does it for you.

- **Sharing isn't the same thing as turning in:** When a student clicks open an assignment to hand in their assignment; they need to click on TURN IN. Sharing an assignment to the Google Classroom is not the same thing as turning in your completed work. Make sure you click on TURN IN to submit your assignment in due time.

- **You will not lose assignments:** Unless you delete it. Any documents you upload to your Google Classroom is only seen between you and the teacher. Any assignments you upload to your Google Drive will be seen on the teachers' Google Drive as well. Your Google Drive is the storage system for Google Classroom and it works the same way for both the teacher as well as the students.

- **Due Dates:** You'd have a harder time explaining to your teacher why you have not submitted your assignment especially since the due dates are continuously shown on an assignment. Assignments that are not due yet are indicated on the class tile on the home page as well as the left of the page late assignments have a particular folder, where the teacher can accurately see the assignments listing from the menu icon on the upper left of the page.

- **Returning an Assignment:** Students working on a Google Document can return at any time to the file that they are working on. Get back to the assignment stream and click on Open and it will take you to a link to the documents that you have on Google Drive. Click on the document and get back right into it. You can also access this file directly from your personal Google Drive. It is the same way you click on any document on your desktop to work on it again. Plus, the side is Google Docs autosaved.

- **Communicating with teachers:** It's either you communicate publicly on Google Classrooms for the entire class to see, or you communicate privately. Communicating privately helps a lot especially for students who are shy and prefer to speak to the teacher directly without the involvement of other classmates. It also helps the teacher to speak privately to address a student's issue on an assignment without making them feel inadequate or that they have not done well.

- **Commenting on Assignments:** Comments on an assignment are viewable by your classmates on Google Classroom when it is made on any assignments uploaded to the app. Students just need to click on 'Add Comments' under an assignment. If students would like to communicate in private, with you, they can leave it on the assignment submission page. Within a specific document, you can use the File Menu and click on

'Email collaborators' to message or link a document to the teacher.

- **Add Additional files to an assignment:** Students and teachers can both add additional files to an assignment. For students, they can add in files that did not come together with a template the teacher gave. You can click on ADD additional files on the assignment submission page again. Links from websites can also be added. Additional files help in the attempt to provide a wholesome blended learning approach in schools because you can add files of different formats and types.

CHAPTER 3:

Benefits of Google Classroom

As a free online learning system, Google Classroom brings various advantages for students and teachers alike. Here are a few of the key reasons that teachers would try it out for.

Ten reasons teachers should try it out here.

Accessibility

Google Classroom is accessible from any desktop, or with any mobile device, irrespective of software, through Google Chrome.

Both data exchanged by students and teachers are kept in a Google Drive Classroom archive.

The Classroom is open to users everywhere. Students should no doubt be talking about faulty computers or hungry pets.

Exposure

The classroom gives students exposure to an online learning system. Most College and University programs also allow applicants to take part in at least one online class.

Exposure at Google Classroom will help students switch to other learning management programs that are common in higher education.

Paperless

Teachers and students will not have to shift excessive amounts of paper as the Classroom is completely paperless. As teachers submit classroom tasks and tests; they are enabled to move concurrently.

Students can complete tasks and assessments straight from the Classroom, and may also hold their job to Travel. Students may have recourse to missed assignments related to absences and will often have certain resources that are possibly needed.

Time Saver

A great time-saver is a classroom. With all the resources saving at one place and getting access to the Classroom at all moments, teachers will have more spare time to perform certain assignments.

While the Classroom is available from a mobile computer, students, and teachers may use their phones and tablets to get active.

Communication

Teachers and students are allowed to send emails, post on the internet, provide private feedback on assignments, and receive job information. Teachers are totally in control of students' feedback and updates. They may also communicate with parents through individual emails or via Classroom email summaries, which include dates and class announcements.

Collaborate

The curriculum provides several opportunities for students to interact together. Within the classroom, teachers will promote online discussions among students and construct group projects. Moreover, students can work together to share Google Docs with teachers.

Engagement

Many digital natives are comfortable with technology and must be more likely to take responsibility and control of using technology. The classroom provides multiple means of rendering learning more engaging and constructive.

It enables teachers to differentiate assignments, integrate videos, and web sites into the classes and build collective community activities.

Differentiation

The teachers can clearly discern learners teaching through the Classroom. Assigning lessons to the entire college, specific students, or classes of students requires just a few required measures while creating a task on a Classwork website.

Feedback

An important aspect of all the training is to give the students positive input. Within the assessment resource at the Classroom, teachers will give each student input on assignments.

Within the rating process, there is also the ability to create a statement bank for future usage. The iOS device Classroom, in turn, lets users annotate work.

Data Analysis

To keep learning effective, instructors will evaluate data from the assessment and ensure the learners understand learning goals. Information from analyses may be forwarded easily to Sheets for storing and review.

CHAPTER 4:

Virtual Classes

Prepare Your Mind

A virtual educator is someone who has to teach day and night as different students live in different parts of the world. When you teach online, no matter what time of day you teach, don't show unnecessary details about your private life to your students.

The important thing here is that you teach with sincerity and show so much interest in the topics you teach. The quality of your teaching is reflected in your delivery.

Your student classroom can be spread from different parts of the world. Your student doesn't care if you had a good night's sleep or a bad day.

Engage your students with positivity from your attitude, voice, and mental attitude. Make sure your students get the best possible learning experience from you.

Being Flexible Is Key

Being flexible is crucial every time you are in front of your virtual audience. You may experience interruptions when information is not well received by your audience. Information cannot be received for various reasons, from technical to cultural. That is why flexibility is part of the solution. You must be able to adapt to the circumstances you experience.

Communicate Regularly and Provide Feedback

Your students can give you relevant feedback that can help move your entire class forward. Your students may have attended the online class more often than most. That experience can help educate you about the pros and cons of your overall online classroom.

In addition to your online students, you can also look for and connect with other online teachers. Keep in mind that education is a 'sharing' field. These connections can be invaluable for your online education development.

You see, online education is an excellent opportunity. The flexibility is an incredible benefit for teachers and students around the world. It is a growing market for virtual teachers and therefore an exciting career development opportunity.

How to Be a Virtual Communicator?

The art and science of communication is an essential part of being human. The exchange of information, thoughts, and ideas from person to person is communication. Humans have developed different communication processes to understand and express each other as the most intelligent animals on Earth. Not only do we have different ways of expressing oral communication; we also have nonverbal communication methods, such as facial expressions, gestures, and body movements.

We have used new technology to expand written and oral communication, which has led to the advent of a new form of communication, virtual communication, which simulates personal communication using technology.

Today, web-based services such as video conferencing and webcams make virtual communication commonplace. The people you talk to may be in the next room, another apartment nearby, or abroad. Today it is used in almost every way of life for family, friends, businesses, and online education.

In the past, writing decorum was considered suitable for electronic messages, now we have adopted a new way of communicating. Texting and messaging have evolved in a very interesting way over time with abbreviations like LOL and emojis making a big impact.

How Do Teachers Communicate Virtually?

Virtual education combines best practices from video production, video conference practices, and traditional teaching methods.

The teacher is often the subject of the video or stream while giving live online instruction. A subject is a person who holds the attention of the audience as an actor on stage. As a virtual teacher, you are not only an actor, but also the director who sets the scene, scripts the part and brings the setting, environment, and all components of a story to life.

Virtual communicators use a combination of oral, non-verbal, and written processes to transfer messages between parties via electronic media. Technology improves the way the subjects align mood, attitude, scene, and mood in ways that would otherwise be lost without being personal.

If you consider your class as a movie stage, you better prepare as a virtual teacher while delivering content in different virtual settings.

As a virtual educator, you need to look for ways in which technology can enhance or complement your students' experience. You can use live video and streaming technology to expand the billboards of your classroom to billions of students online.

Virtual teachers use the best of their environment, comparable to physical settings. Teachers in the classroom need to understand how to control the room. Getting and keeping your audience's attention is always a challenge for virtual teachers. Regardless of the circumstances, physical, or virtual; teachers are responsible for distributing instructions, guiding their research, and building their confidence.

Be a Better Virtual Communicator

Below are the main ways you can become a better virtual communicator:

Use different ways to express yourself

Virtual communication is not just about video and audio. As you can see on TV and film, each specific scene can dramatically change the mood, perception, and subsequent look at the actors' actions.

You are central to the classroom. Communicate a positive, upbeat attitude, and happy emotions to create a stimulating mental mood among your audience, in the classroom or on a webcam, TV, or stage.

Practicing the correct posture is key when standing in front of the camera. Make sure your back is straight and upright; your chin should be perpendicular to the floor and level with the camera.

Get instant feedback

The good thing about networking today is that it enables two-way communication. You can give and receive direct viewer feedback on the effectiveness and relevance of your material and delivery.

Feedback channels are great ways to capture your audience's thoughts and feelings. Feedback channels such as testimonials, reviews, and customer satisfaction departments are typically used by companies to correct courses and/or improve products.

To improve your teaching quality and to support your students; you need to set up feedback channels at the beginning of your interaction.

Feedback channels in a virtual educational environment are likely to follow the example of any company or private institution. Customer reviews, thoughts, and constructive criticism should be welcomed by virtual teachers. You can concentrate the feedback by creating online surveys that are integrated into your courses.

In addition, feedback channels are created between customers and brands to provide real-time customer feedback. But always remember that feedback isn't always about direct comments, surveys, or specific to your development.

For example:

"I normally have a class with many active participants. However, when discussing the difference between past and present, no one took part in the online activity I had prepared. The change in behavior was a red flag. The content provided was ineffective or the way it was introduced.

Note which student actions in the previous example were considered the norm and how often that norm changed. Use the input to act accordingly in class and prepare for lessons. The teacher immediately identified a change in behavior regarding her instruction and a necessary change. We will bring up various feedback channels in this text.

One of the most typical feedback channels for virtual teachers today is electrical messages such as instant messaging (chat), texting, or emails. Anytime you can establish one-on-one communication with your students; it helps build trust and honesty.

Use exciting and eye-catching activities

You need to use unique and relevant technology resources to get your messages across, just like in any traditional classroom. Not all ideas will stimulate your audience, this is a trial and error method. Therefore, choose carefully and keep up with unique ways to keep students interested in the learning materials while online.

Attention and motivation can be easily influenced by audiences of all ages. The content you use will compete with current event alerts, specialized social media notifications, and a wave of free streaming entertainment. How will you compete? Why does your audience want to participate in the learning process that is currently taking place? How can the audience communicate with you to stay involved? One way to get your students' attention and familiarize them with participation is to use virtual icebreakers. An icebreaker is an approach you can use to initiate conversations and remove embarrassment and barriers between your audience. Generally, icebreakers occur after introductions. You could use one before classwork puts everyone in a learning mood. Below are good examples of virtual icebreakers you can use:

- Find an activity that students can participate in by using items that members of the audience can find at home. This makes the activity cheap and fun for everyone.

- Interactive games and software where the public can participate in the promotion.

- Relevant songs and music (in whatever form).

- Ask the audience a question to respond via chat, comment, etc.

- Share your screen—some activities may not match the size of your class, but you can show your screen and participate in a game for them.

- All students choose topics for discussion. Find out what concerns them. (Note: This changes the spotlight and gives your audience the opportunity to be topics in class).

- Getting to know each other is a good icebreaker; introductions can be as long or short as you like.

Games are an excellent way to learn. Learning through fun and games has been receiving the undivided attention of the many target groups for a long time.

Integrate independent research as part of learning

Your audience should learn and understand how to use the tools they have on hand. A goal of modern researchers is to develop self-sufficient researchers.

You will find a wide variety of resources spread over the Internet. Your goal is to help your students decipher all this data. Knowing how to search the Internet for the best and worst sources of information is critical to gaining reliable and accurate knowledge of any topic. Incorrect information is prevalent on the internet. We help our virtual students to become independent researchers in their school work.

Maximize the time you have from start to finish

Don't waste screen time. As with any live production, the set is prepared before the cameras start rolling. Before you turn on the webcam, make sure you are as willing as possible to present your lesson, provide feedback, and answer questions.

Use the time you have with your students effectively. Our world is moving at a very fast pace. Respecting your audience's time is a golden rule for any teacher. In addition, punctuality and timeliness is a requirement for any virtual teacher who uses the Internet to complement the classroom environment. Remember that good, engaging alternative learning materials will help fill in the time to the end of the lesson. It also helps to strengthen the material given during the lesson. For example, keep flashcards, games, video, or some relevant learning material on hand for last-minute fill-ins. There will be times when you have planned a lesson and the planned material goes through faster than expected.

CHAPTER 5:

Getting Started with Google Classroom

While classrooms become more paperless, teachers need to find solutions for homework sharing, classroom management, student communication, and so on.

More and more teachers are coming to Google Classroom for smooth virtual classes that focus less on technology and more on teaching. You don't need to be a tech professional to lead this department.

Before you can make Google Classroom a part of your teaching experience, you need to make sure that you download the Google Apps for Education. This is a pretty simple process to go through and have work for you, but there are a few steps that you will need to work on first.

First, there are a few rules for who can get on the Google Classroom app. Any student, parent, or alumni group that has been registered as a 501(c) (3) can get on the Google Classroom app. Also, any accredited or non-profit K through 12 learning institutions can use this as well. You may want to consider talking to your administrator to see if this is a service that is already offered through your school or not.

Once you have checked in on this part, you will need to go through the following steps to sign up for the app:

- You will want to start by going to the sign-up form for the Apps for Education. You will be able to find it at https://www.google.com/a/signup/?enterprise_product=GOOGLE.EDU#

- Once you are on this page, you can fill the form in and then click on the Next button.

- From here, you will provide your institution's domain. If this isn't available, you can go through and purchase a new domain to help you get this started.

- Then click on Next and provide the rest of the information that is needed so that you can become an admin.

- Make sure to read through the Agreement before accepting and finishing the sign-up.

You may want to consider doing this a little bit early, like before school starts, because it can take up to two weeks before Google is done reviewing the application. After this time frame, you are going to receive your own acceptance form when the application is successful. You will now be able to verify your own domain as well as add addresses, mail integration, apps, and contacts to start using this. Keep in mind that you will not need to do this for each class, but you only need to go through this and do it one time. Once you are in, you will be able to assign different classrooms and have more than one in place under the same account.

From here, you will need to work on downloading the Google Classroom App. You will be able to go to the App Store and get this one just by looking for Google Classroom, or you can just visit Google Play and find it as well. Once you have downloaded this particular app; you will need to choose to sign in as the teacher. It is also possible to download an extension or a bookmark-like app that will work on Google Chrome. You just need to visit the Chrome Store to install all of this.

There are a few ways that you can install the Google Classroom App so that you can use it for your own needs. If you are considered the administrator; you will be able to install this extension by using the following steps:

- Visit the Google Admin Console.

- From here you will click on Chrome Management and then User Settings.

- Then you will be able to select the organizational unit that you would like to work with from here.

- Now you can click on Apps & Extension before clicking on Force Installed Apps & Extension. When you get to this point, click on Manage Force Installed App.

- Inside this tab, you will click on Chrome Web Store and then look for the series of letters that don't seem to make sense and click on those. If you can't find that, you can click on Share to Classroom.

- Now click the Add button that is right next to your extension before hitting save.

These steps are only if you are going to be the administrator. If you are using the Google Classroom through your educational institution, you will not need to go through the steps above because someone else will go through and do it. The steps that you will need to go through as a teacher, and that your students will need to go through as well, include:

Visit g.co/sharetoclassroom

When you get here, you can click on Add to Chrome and then click on the Add button.

From here, you can click on the icon that is next to the extension. You will need to make sure that you are signed in with Google before you do all of this.

And that is all that you will need to do to make sure that Google Classroom is downloaded for you and that you can use it for your classroom and your teaching experience. Since this is such a popular platform to work with, it is likely that your school already has this available for you to use for your classes, or they will be interested in learning more about it.

Now your class is ready! At least it is there, and anyone can access it. There are a few other things that need to be done before you go out.

Create your first project or create a message. You can share your first ad in Stream, or you can go to class. Click the "Create" button and share your first assignment in Google Classroom. Remember to count your projects. Make it easy for your students to see who comes first because you are unable to organize your tasks manually. However, you can move projects up. Click on the title to see if any students have completed the project and provide grades and feedback. Then you can give your students the tasks so they can start changing again.

Add teaching material to your project/class. Add content from Google Drive, or add a video from YouTube, files from your computer, links, and more. You can get these settings right on the right day. If you just want to share a presentation on your non-project-related class, go to the "about" file. Here you can add some teaching material such as slides, interesting articles, and examples. Log in to the drive directory. Each time you create a new class, Google Classroom Drive creates a folder for that category. You can access the folder by going to all your class tiles. In each tile, you will find icons for the folder. Click on it, and you're in the folder. You can also add class material here. All of your students' tasks are automatically filled into the Google Drive folder, so you can get them back anytime you want.

CHAPTER 6:

Navigate Google Classroom

Navigation and Some Other Settings of Google Classroom

When you sign in to GC there is much to try for. You will have to know how to do navigate first. The very first page you will see, is the homepage of the Classroom, shows all of the classes that you have made or joined.

The Classroom Homepage

Class Tile: It displays the class name and student number on Google Drive, and also a link to the grade book and folder for the class files.

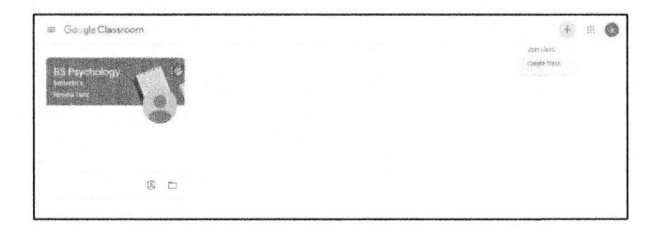

Creating or joining a class: Press the + to create a new class, or use a class code to join a class.

Google Apps: Jump into the suite for another Google app.

The app you selected will open in a fresh browser tab.

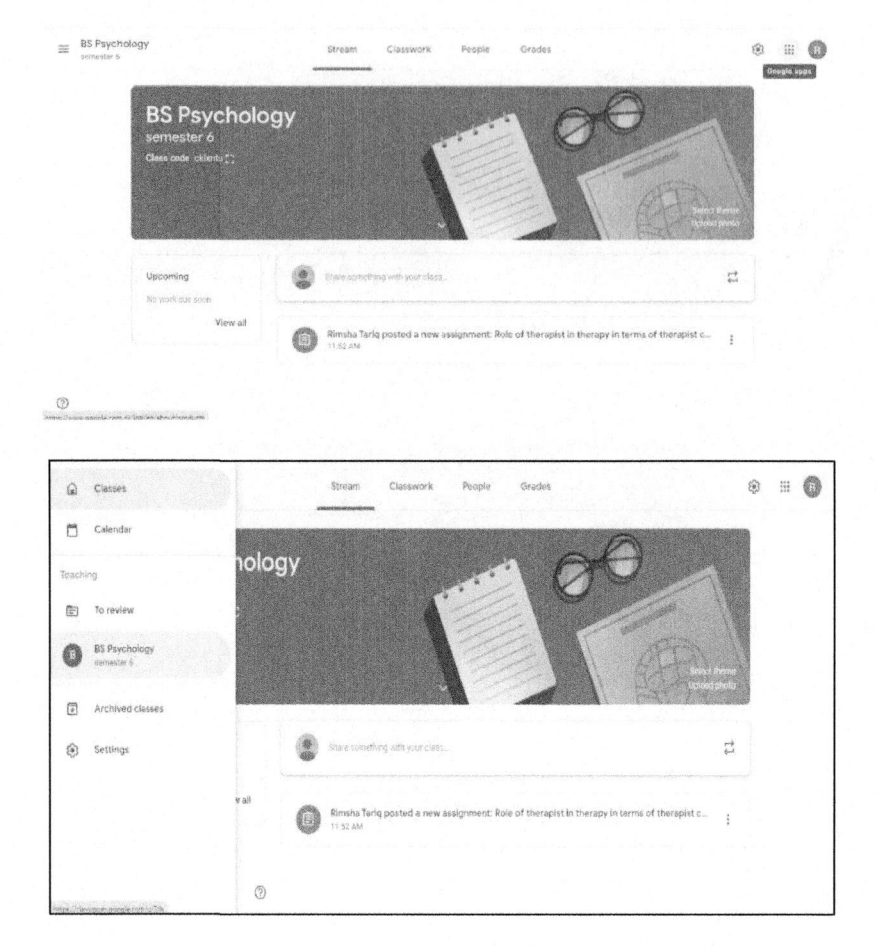

Menu: Provides options for adjusting viewpoints, switching to a class, or altering settings.

Google Account: Change settings of your Google Account by clicking on your image.

You can open your Google Account tab, sign out, or attach another Google Account.

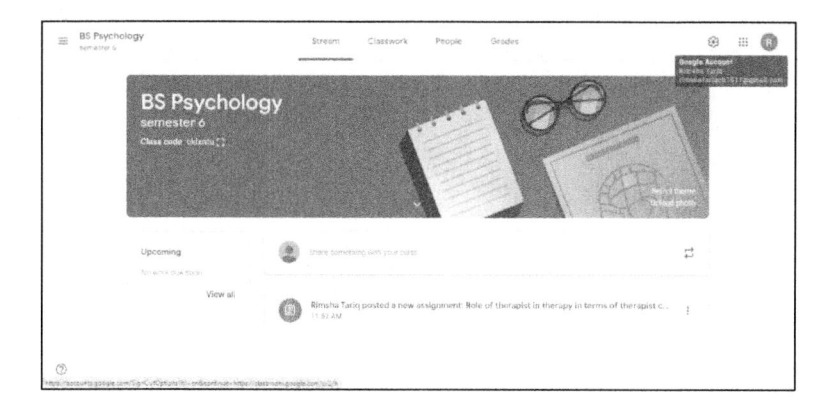

Sign: To see what's new, give your suggestions, inquire, or get support.

Google Classroom menu

Active Classes: The menu here shows the participating courses. Move to a class easily by clicking on them.

To-do: See the To-do page for an overview of questions and assignments across all of your classes. You will search by class and just display the job within a single class.

Calendar: Record class schedules for assignments, queries, and activities in the class calendar. You and the students will display a calendar image of the job for every semester.

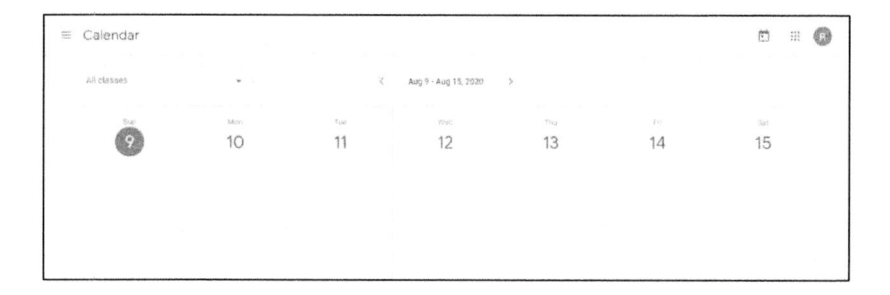

Classes: You have to see the GC homepage which displays the tile format of your classes that are active.

Archived Classes: Access the classes you were attending. Restore these groups or uninstall them right here.

Settings: Manage your account settings, change your profile, and adjust the email, comment, and classwork notifications. The settings available are Google Classroom wide settings affecting all classes that you are teaching.

How to Navigate Your Class?

To access a class click on the class page.

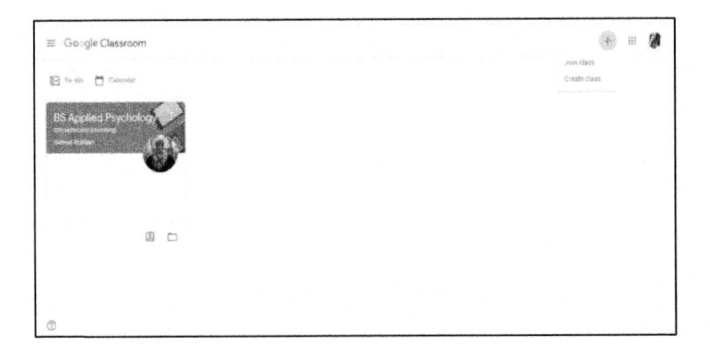

Upon joining a class, you can see the class code which students need to use, as well as four top tabs.

To jump to a class area, click a tab at the top of the page.

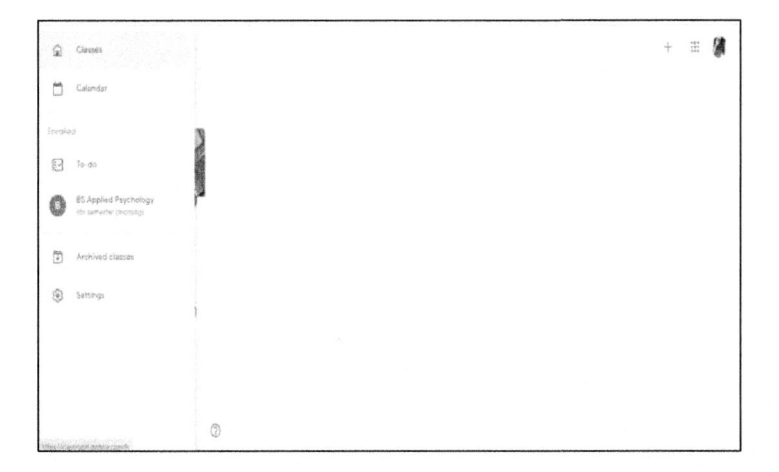

Classwork: That is where the submissions, queries, and class materials are made. In addition, to retain the Classwork page structured; you can create themes.

You can create a topic, for example, one for homework, one for classwork, and another for the project. All like work will be structured under your assigned topic.

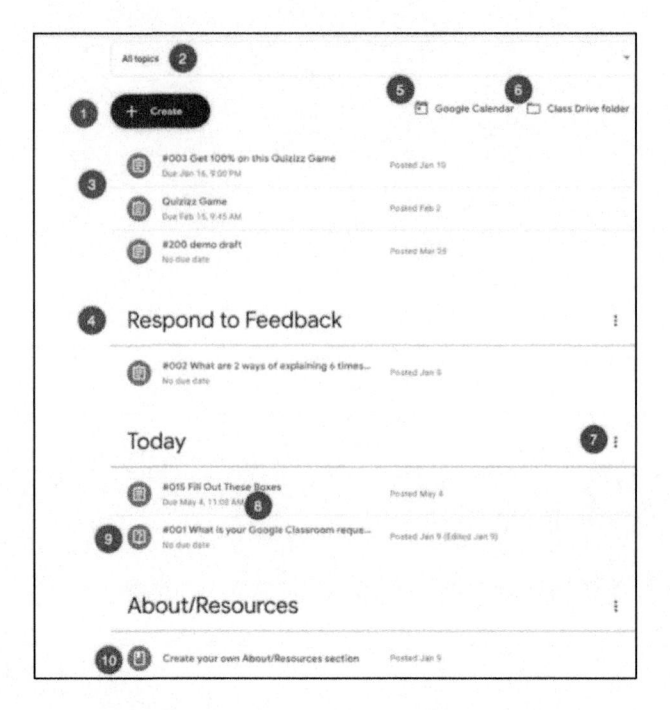

1. Create assignments.

2. Filter for topics.

3. Assignments without a topic.

4. Topic headings.

5. Class Google Calendar.

6. Class Google Drive folder.

7. Three Dots More menu for the topic.

8. Due Date and time.

9. Question assignment posted.

10. Materials posted.

Stream: This is a prime location for viewing announcements and class posts. That always occurs on the Stream as it is applied to the classwork. A list of submissions with the given upcoming dues dates is displayed on the left-hand side of the Stream page in the Next area.

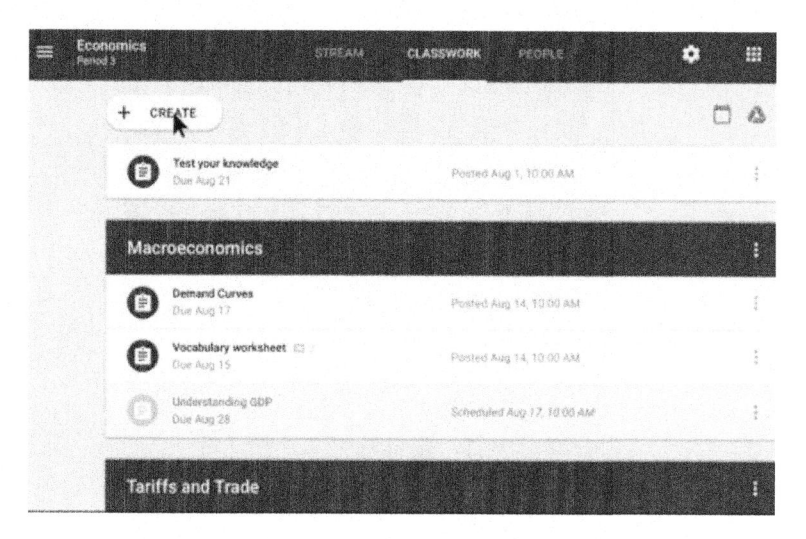

Grades: It includes viewing, grading, and returning assignments. You see both individual scores for students as well as the average class.

People: This tab holds a list of classes for both instructors and class co-workers. Further people can also be added to the class from here.

1. Add the co-teacher.

2. Via email invite a student.

3. Select all the students.

4. Email all the guardians.

5. Sort by the first name.

6. Select an individual student.

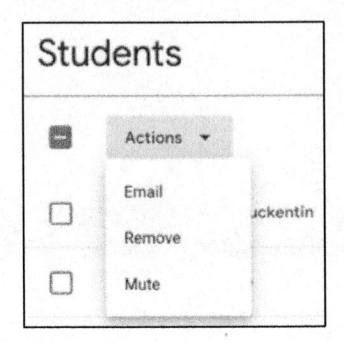

7. **Actions:** Email the selected student(s). Remove the selected students. Mute the selected students from posting to the class Stream.

You Can Handle or Change Class Details

Upon building a class, you can display or alter the specifics of your class. Facts of the curriculum include:

- General information, like class name, room number, and section

- The video meeting link in class

- Settings to your Stream tab for articles

- Your category code

The class settings can be updated on your Preferences tab. If you have various segments of the same class, modifications to a single class don't apply to others.

Edit a Class Section, Name, Room, Description, or Subject

A class name is needed. If you modify the class name, this will not automatically update the title of the class Drive folder. To update the name of the folder goes to your Drive class folder.

Go to the classroom.google.com.

Then click Settings and then click Class.

The class name is entered automatically.

Enter your changes under Class Details, and click Save.

Edit your class. In the student view, blank fields do not show.

Reset, Copy or Turn off The Class Code

When you build a class, Classroom generates a file for the lesson automatically.

You can reset it if the students have difficulties with the class code.

You can enable the code if you don't want to see new students joining your class. You can activate this at any time.

Once a class code is reset or activated, Classroom must generate some new code for your class.

The preceding code works no longer.

Then, go to the classroom.google.com.

Next, click Settings and then click Class.

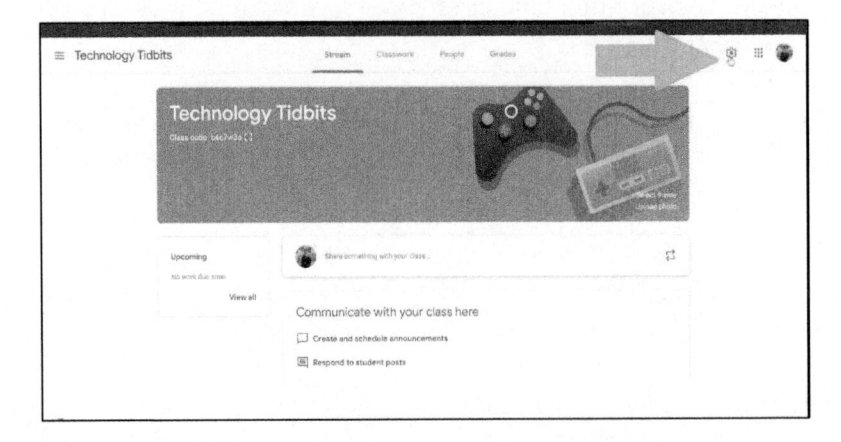

Under General, click the Down arrow next to the code of a class, and then choose an option:

Tap on Display to display the address.

Click Reset to reset the Code.

Click Disable or Activate to turn the code either off or on.

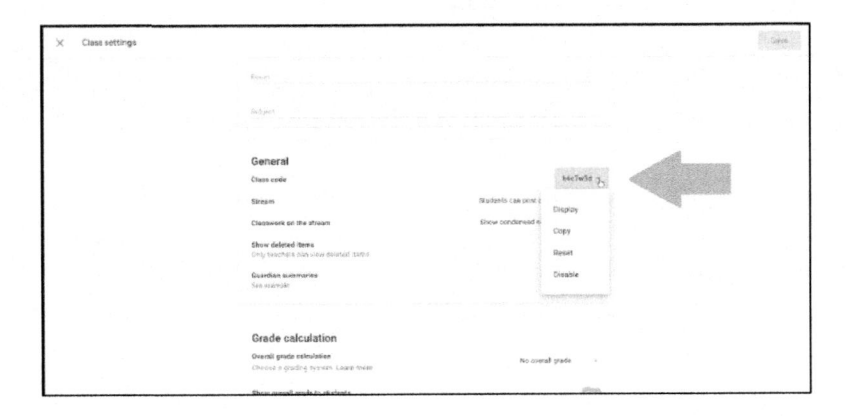

Click on Copy to copy code.

Then just click Save.

Choose How Classwork Notifications Show On the Stream Page

You may select how the Stream page shows alerts for your Classwork updates, and what information the alerts contain.

Go to the classroom.google.com.

Then click Settings and then click Class.

Click the Down arrow next to the Classwork on the page, and then pick an option:

Display details and attachments—students should see an updated update screen.

Show simplified alerts—Students display updates without information and attachments.

Hide Notifications—the Stream tab contains not any Classwork Notifications.

Click the Save button. Only teachers see totals turned in, graded, and assigned to an assignment.

To Note Deleted Student Posts

You will see any of the posts and comments a student-created and erased afterward. Go to the classroom.google.com.

Then click Settings and then click Class.

Under General press the On or Off switch next to Show Deleted Objects.

Click the Save button.

CHAPTER 7:

How to Set-up Google Classroom

Creating and Setting Classes

Getting into Google Classroom is really easy. You just have to access by logging in to classroom.google.com you can use your personal email or email specifically for your profession.

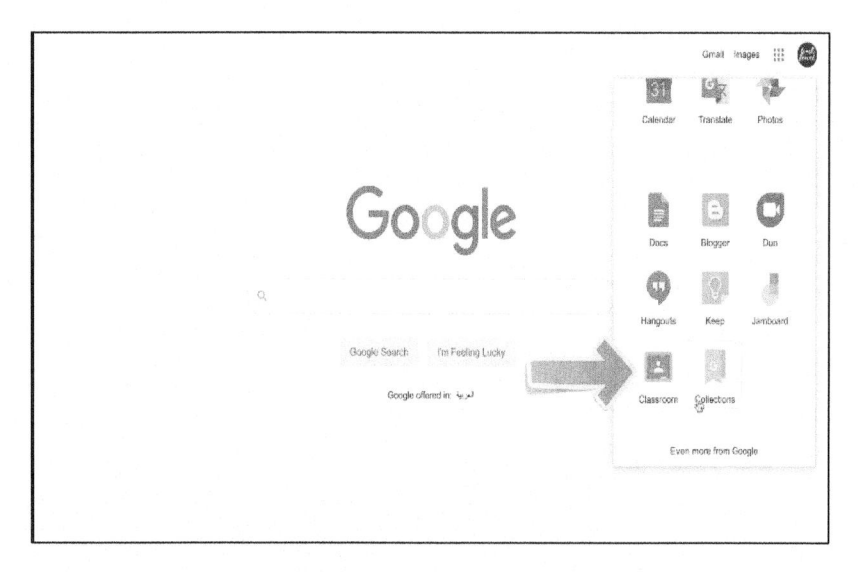

By the upper right portion, there is an icon of "+," and by pressing that; we can create a class if we are a teacher or join a class if we are a student.

To create a class, we can choose a class, sector, subject, and classroom name.

Because of this, students would be able to identify their classes and subjects easily.

From there, the class would then be created and the Class Code would be available that can be used to invite students.

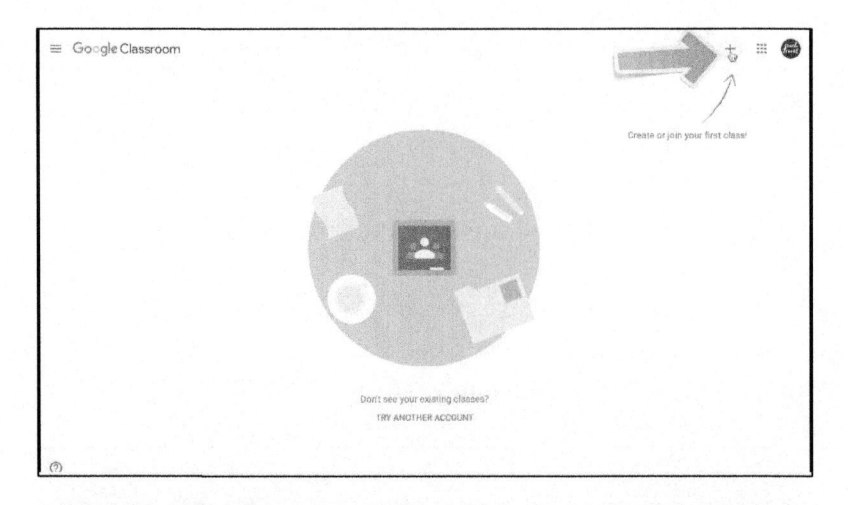

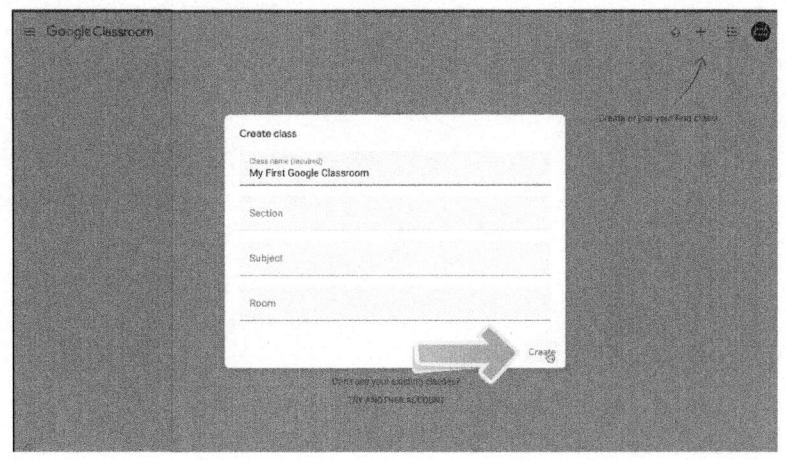

Inviting Your Students on Google Classroom

There are two ways you can invite students into your Google Classroom: by displaying class code or by inviting them directly.

Well, to invite students by class code, log into your Google Classroom. Select a classroom where you would like to invite your students to. Your class code is displayed right underneath your name, click on Display, and make sure that the class code is visible to your students. You can either project it onto the screen or simply write it on the board.

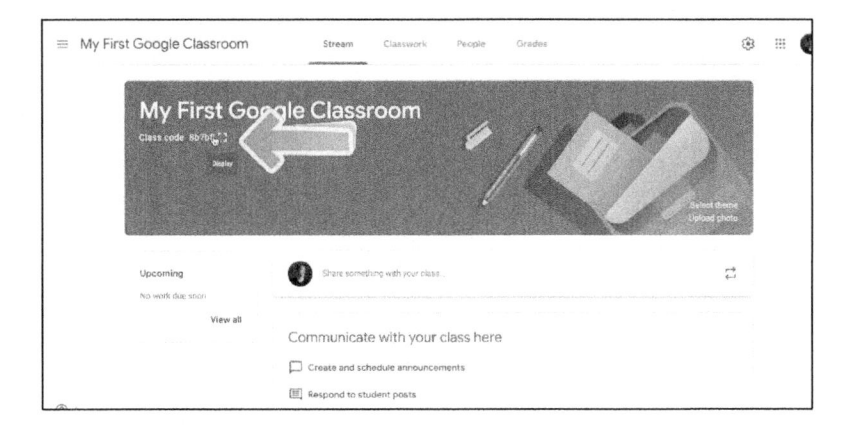

Instruct your students to sign into Google using their school Gmail accounts. Instruct your students to go to Google classroom, click the plus button in the top right corner. This is the time where they will insert a class code. Once they finished, click join. That's it; a student has successfully joined your Google Classroom.

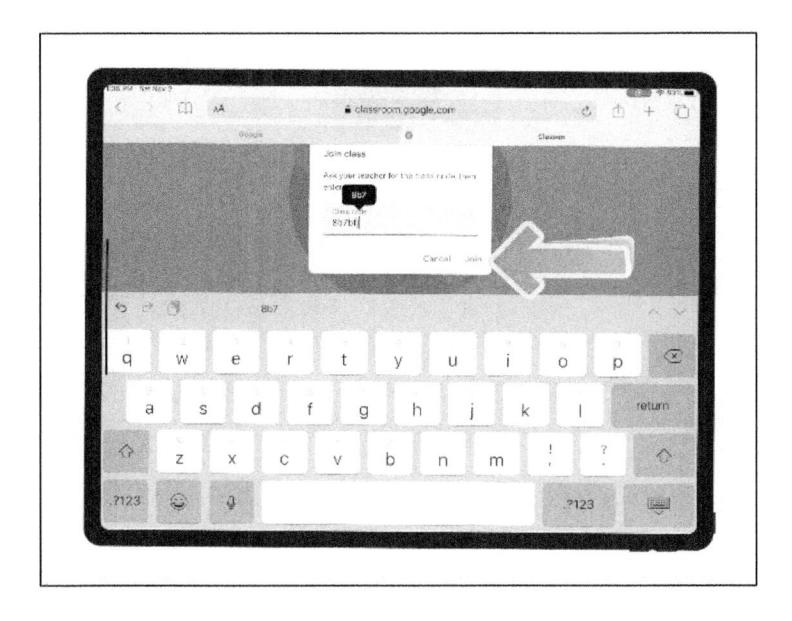

pag. 148

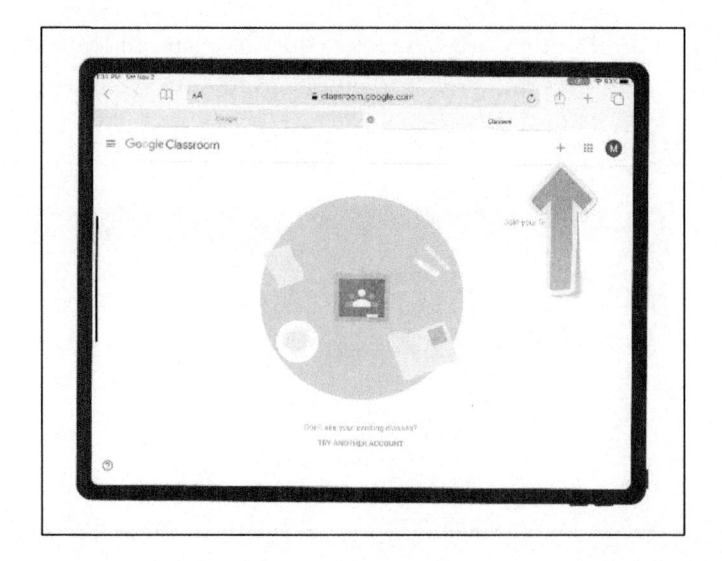

A direct invitation is another way to populate your Google Classroom. To do that, open your Google classroom, select a class where you would like to invite your students to go to the "people" tab. Find sign invite students and click on it. This is the field where you will paste or type names or emails of the students who you would like to invite. Once you've finished, click invite. Once the invitation has been sent; you will see the name of the students grayed out. They have received the invitation but have not joined a class yet.

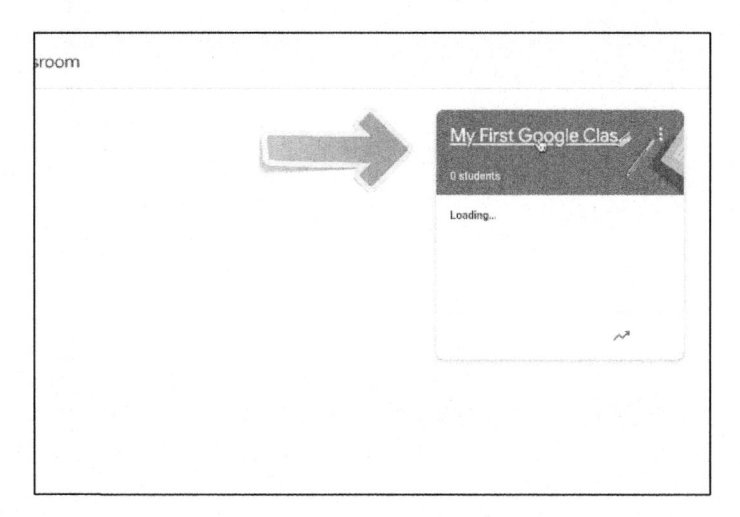

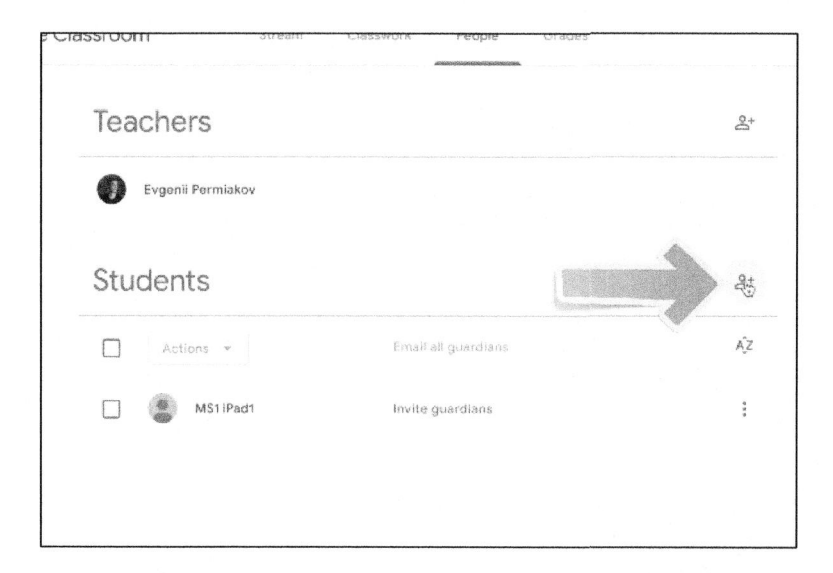

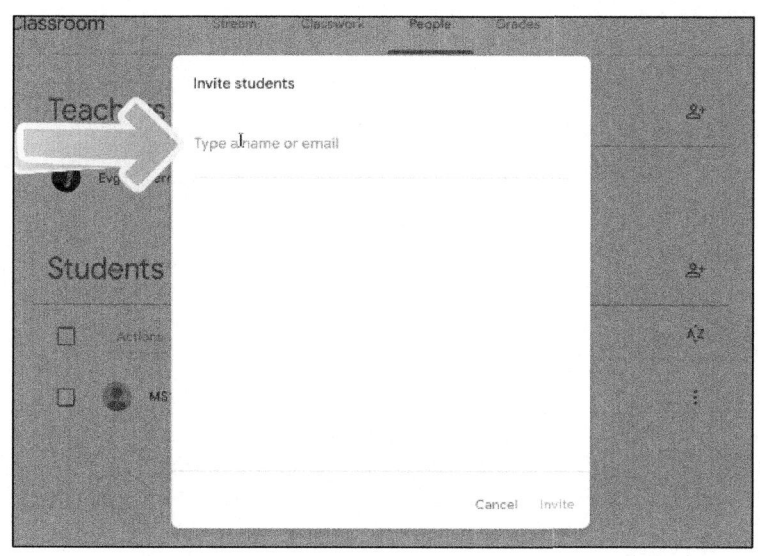

Instruct your students to login into Google using their school accounts. Once they've logged in, instruct them to go to Google Classroom.

Once there, they should be able to see a Google Classroom, which you have invited them to. In my case, it's my first Google Classroom. The final step they need to take is to click join.

That's it. Your student has successfully joined your Google Classroom by direct invitation.

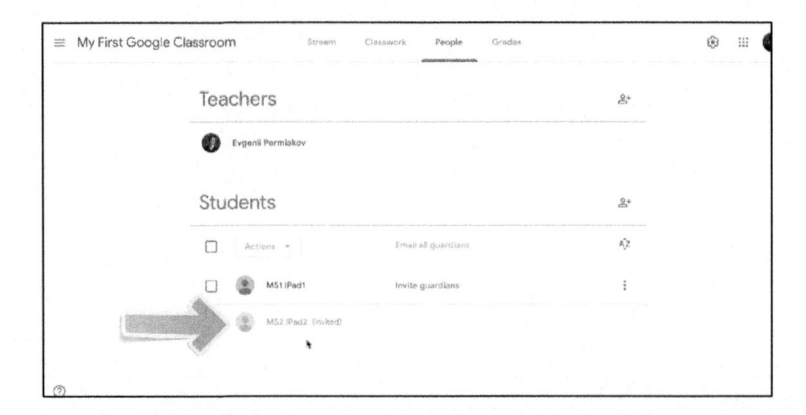

In the teachers' view to see what has changed and name that used to be grayed out is now solid black. If the name still appears light gray, it means that a student has not yet accepted your invitation.

How to Create and Collect Assignments/Tasks from Students

To create an assignment, go to classwork and click 'Create assignment'. Give your assignment a title, type up instructions for your students. Select whether your assignment will be ungraded or graded. Select a due date for your assignment.

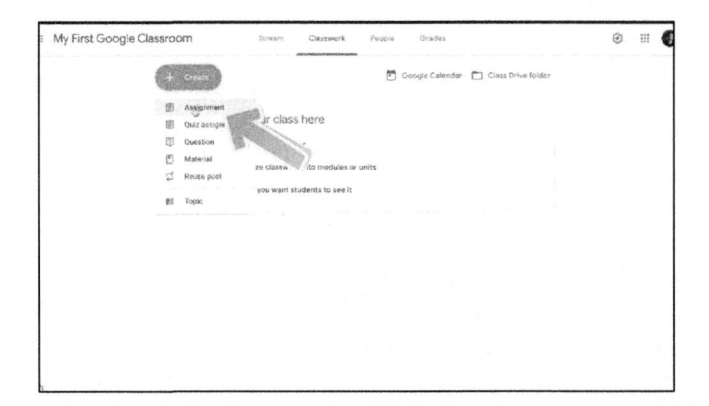

There are four kinds of supplementary materials that you can attach to your assignment. The first one is an attachment from your computer or a file; the second one is a file from your Google Drive. The third one is a YouTube video clip. The fourth is linked to any resource found on the internet.

Finally, I would like my students to be able to reflect on all the materials they've watched. For this purpose, I created a Google Doc. So I will click on the second icon and select a Google Doc that I've recently created for this assignment. Select the file from your Google Drive and click add. One important thing you need to remember when assigning Google Docs to your classes is to select the appropriate sharing type wherein the students can view the file; students can edit the file, and make a copy for each student.

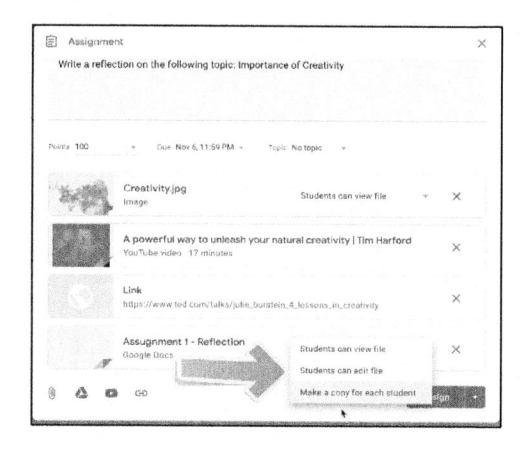

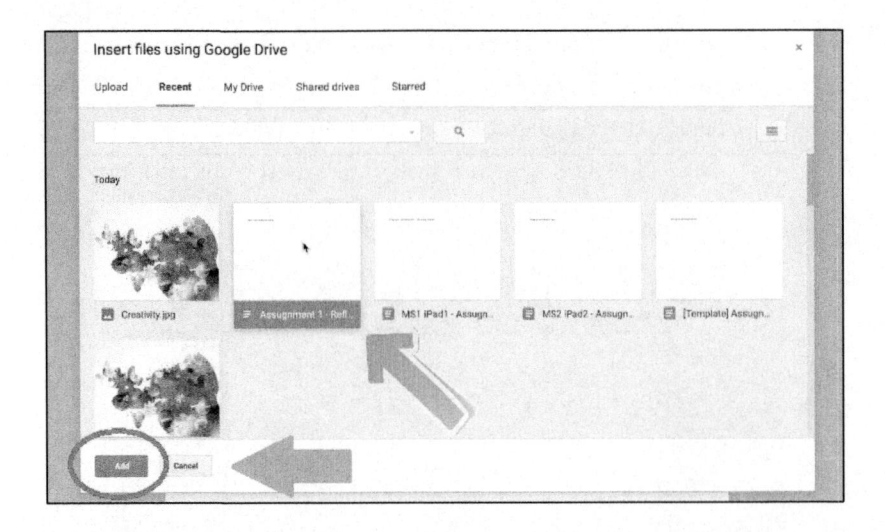

How to Use Question

The first thing you need to do is to go to classwork from your Google Classroom home screen. From there, select Create, select question. This is how we start a discussion board.

The first thing we need to think about is what it is that we want our students to talk about. And this is going to be our question. Well, in my case, I want my students to do discuss a video clip I found on YouTube about 'creativity'. So, this is going to be my question 'share your insights about the attached video', I'm going to click on YouTube sign and attach the video clip that I would like my students to discuss, share, insights, select the clip, click Add. So, I have my question. I have my clip here. And the other thing we need to select is how the students will answer this question. We have two options. We can either accept short answers or multiple choices. Well, in our case, we want to start a discussion board. So short answer makes more sense.

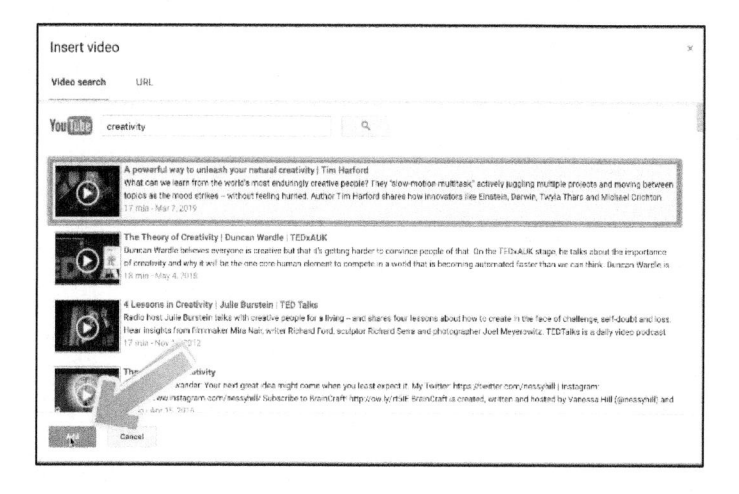

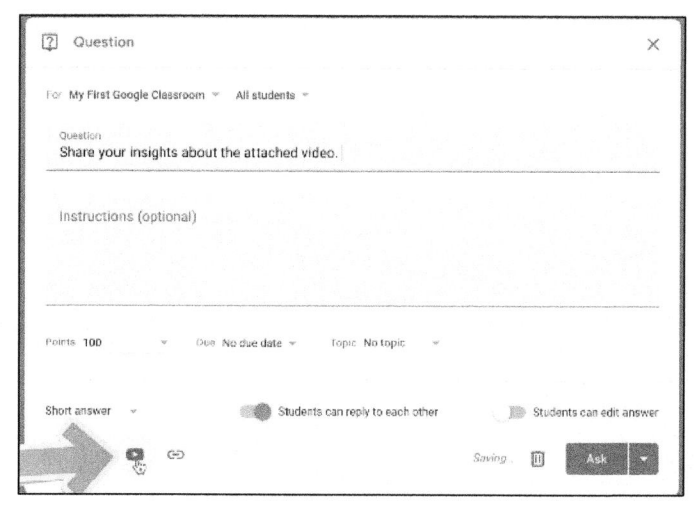

Make sure you enable students to reply to each other and students can edit the answer. This option lets students go back and edit the answers after they've been posted in case they've made a mistake, they can go back and edit. Select classes that you want to assign this question to. We can either ask now, in this case, the assignment will post it right away. We can schedule this assignment for later use, or we can save as draft and maybe ask it later or edit it later. In my case, I'm going to ask it now.

After you've asked your question; it's going to appear onto your classwork or in your stream.

The question can be found right at the top, and I can do three things. I can add a class comment, I can type my answer, or I can add a private comment. And these three things are slightly different from each other.

The question was to share my insights about the video attached. So, my insight would be this video is great.

I'm going to click turn in.

And you will notice that once I've turned in, I can now see classmate's answers if I click on it. I can also see how many replies I have right here.

How to Use Evaluation Tool/Rubrics

If we go to the assignment, you will see a new sign has been added to the user interface to the right of the topic.

The first thing you need to do is create a title because I don't have any rubrics, I'm going to create a rubric from scratch.

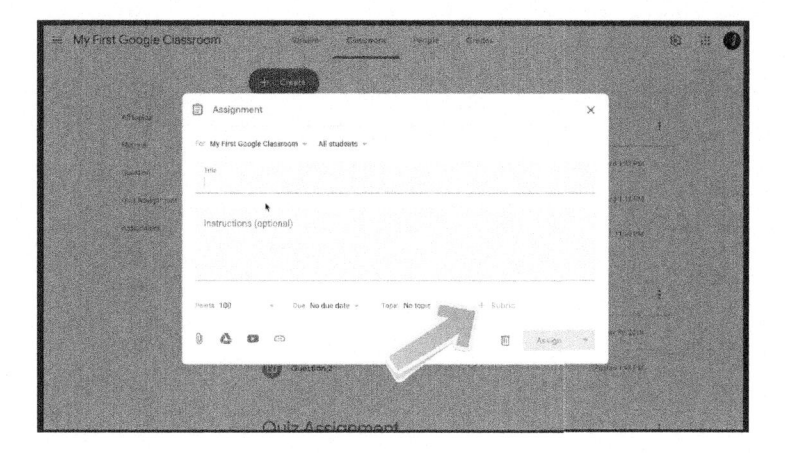

I'm going to be using this rubric for grading student tests. So, my first criteria are going to be word choice. I'm going to assign three points for level three. And this is going to be a description, accurate use of vocabulary. My second level is going to cost three points, it is going to be level two, and the description will be the average use of vocabulary. My third level is going to give the student one point; it's going to be level one, and the description will be a poor use of vocabulary. To add a level, we click on the plus button to the leader level; we need to click on three dots and delete level.

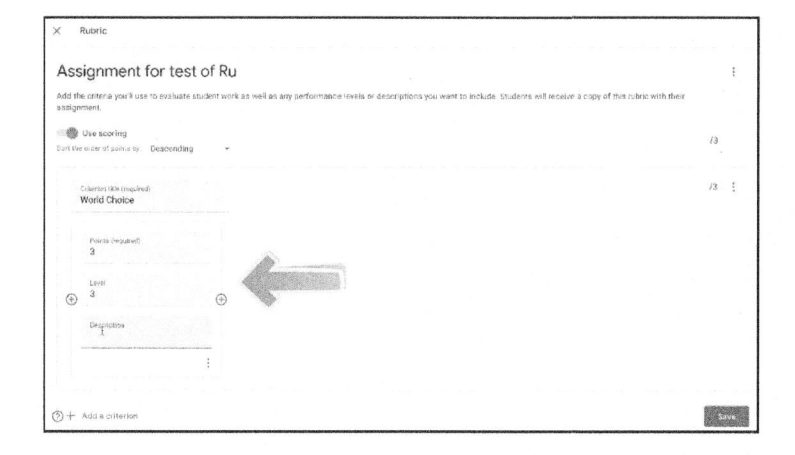

So, my first criteria is ready, I can add a new criteria and if I click that, a new field will be generated for another criteria or what I can do I can duplicate this criteria and just change word choice. I will change it to grammar and tweak my description a little bit at first description will be accurate use of vocabulary.

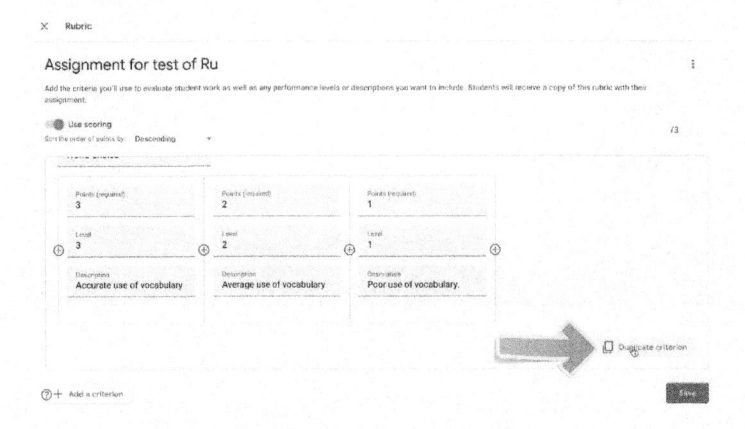

The second description is going to be average; I can duplicate the grammar and choose 'Opinion'. The first level is going to work for point, then three, two, and one. Google rubrics automatically generate the top score. I have three points in word choice, three points in grammar, and four points and opinion, which gives me 10 points. Once my rubric is ready, I'm going to click Save.

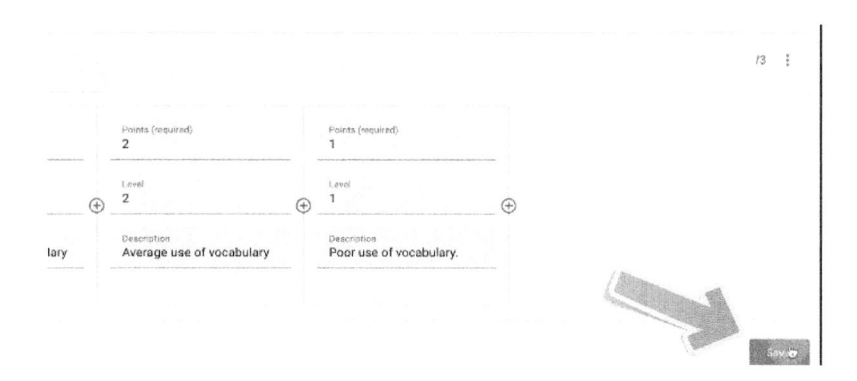

Once you save the rubric; it will be viewable in the assignment, you can click on the rubric, and then it will appear. You have an option to clear the criteria, expand them one by one, or expand them all at once. Once your assignment is ready, click 'assign'. The assignment has been generated.

So from the teacher screen, click on 'turned in' and see the student's submission. My rubric will appear on the right-hand side of my screen. I can expand each level and market accordingly. So, what we've done right now, we've looked at student work, and we've marked it at the same time using our rubric, you will notice that Google rubric has generated the total score of seven out of 10. Based on the levels that we have selected. What it didn't do, however, it didn't transfer the rubric

pag. 158

score into the grade. Google's rubric automatically transfers the rubric score to the final grade.

Use Stream

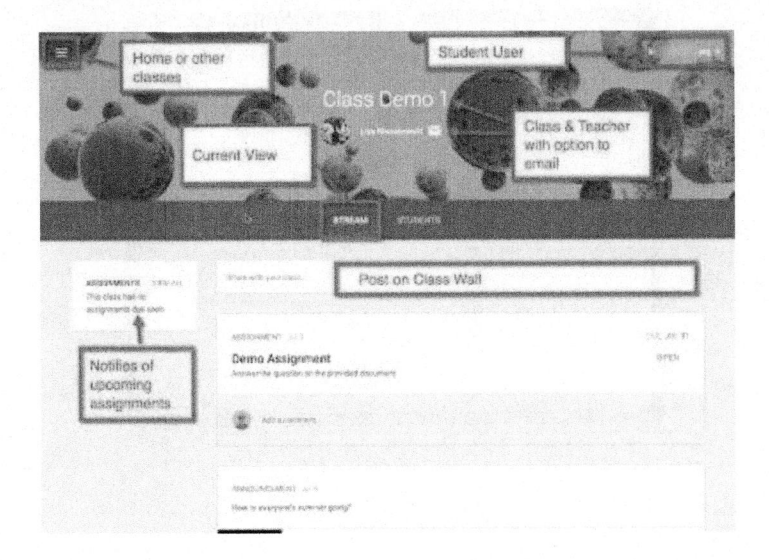

Here are some things you can do in streaming:

- **Post**—you can post your thoughts about certain information and even post your question in the stream of your class.

Examples:

What was our last discussion all about?

- **Comment**—you could respond to people who posted and comment about it.

We talked about addition in Mathematics.

- **Reply**—this is a response directly to the person who commented, especially in your own post

Example: commenter's name. Thanks!

Copy a Course

One of the nice things that a teacher will be able to do with Google Classroom is that they can take some of the posts that they used before, in another class or in a preceding class, and then reuse them a bit. This can be announcements, assignments, and even questions from their preceding classes to help them keep up with the work, especially if the information still works with this current class. For the students, it is possible to go through and see some of the old classes that they were in. This can be helpful if you need to evaluate something that is inside of the older class or you want to get ahold of some papers or discussions that you want to use from a past semester. You just need to go through some of your past archived classes to find what you would like.

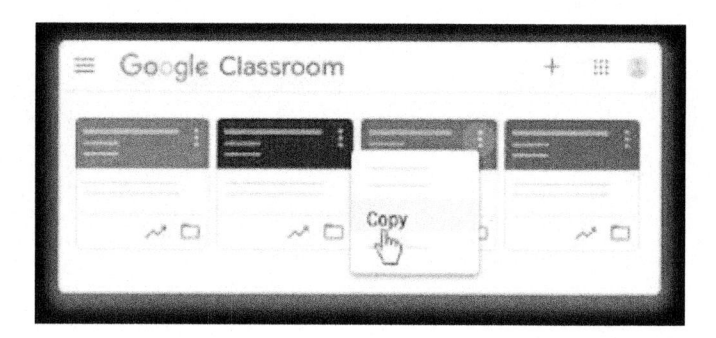

CHAPTER 8:

How to Set Due Date, Manage Homework, and Assignments?

Assignments are a useful tool on Google Classroom for delivering, tracking, and also grading student submissions. Even submissions that are non-electronic can also be tracked using the Assignments tool.

Add an Assignment

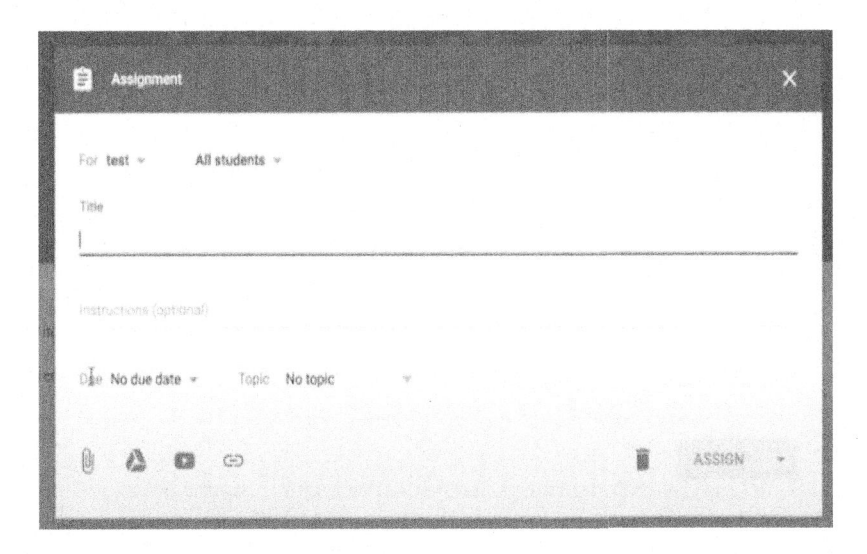

Creating an Assignment

- Open www.classroom.google.com.
- At the top, click on "Class" and open "Classwork."

- Also, click on "Create" and click on "Assignment."

- Input the title and necessary instructions.

Inputting grade category

- Click the drawdown on "Grade Category."

- Select "Category."

- Edit the following (Optional).

- Click "Grades" to edit the grades page.

- Click "Instructions" to compose the Assignment.

- Click "Classwork" to create a homework, quiz, and test.

Change the point value

- Click the drawdown below points.

- Create a new point value or click "ungraded."

Edit due date or Time

- Click on the drawdown below "Due."

- Click on the dropdown on "No due date."

- Fix date on the Calendar.

- Create due Time by clicking Time, input a time adding AM, or PM.

Add a topic

- Click on the drawdown below Topic.

- Click on "Create Topic" and input the topic name.

- Click on an existing topic to select it.

Insert Attachments

File

- Click on "Attach."

- Search for the file and select it.

- Click "Upload."

Drive

- Click on "Drive."

- Search for the item and click it.

- Click "Add."

YouTube

- Click on YouTube.

- Type in the keyword on the search bar and click search.

- Select the video.

- Click "Add."

Link

- Click on Link.

- Select the URL.

- Click on "Add link."

You can delete an attachment

- Click removes or the cross sign beside it.

You can also determine the number of students that interacts with the Attachment:

- Click on the drawdown besides the "Attachment."

- Select the required option.

- Students can View File—this implies that students are allowed to read the data but cannot edit it.

- Students can edit the file—this means students can write and share the same data.

- Make a personal copy of each student—this means students can have their transcript with their name on the file and can still have access to it even when turned in until the teacher return it to them.

Note: If you encounter an issue like, no permission to attach a file, click on copy. This will make the Classroom make a copy, which is attached to the Assignment and saved to the class Drive folder.

Add a Rubric

You must have titled the Assignment before you create a rubric.

- Click the "Add" sign beside Rubric.

- Click on "Create rubric."

- Turn off scoring by clicking the switch to off, besides the Use scoring.

- Using scoring is optional, click "Ascending or Descending" beside the Sort the order of points.

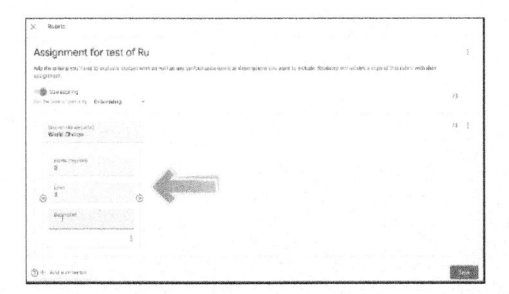

Note: using scoring, gives you the room to add a performance level in any with the levels arranged by point value automatically.

- You can input Criterion like Teamwork, Grammar, or Citations. Click the criterion title.

- Add Criterion description (Optional). Click the Criterion description and input the description.

Note: You can add multiple performance level and Criterion.

- Input points by entering the number of points allotted.

Note: The total rubric score auto-updates as points are added.

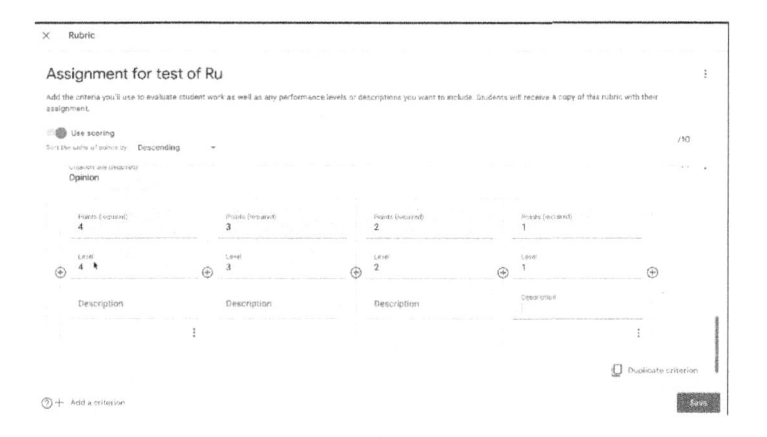

- Add A level title, input titles to distinguish performance level, e.g., Full Mastery, Excellent, Level A.

- Add a Description, input expectations for each performance level.

- Rearrange Criterion by clicking "More" and select "Up or Down."

- Click "Save" on the right corner to save Rubric.

pag. 168

Reuse Rubric

- Click on the "Add" sign beside "Rubric."

- Click "Reuse Rubric."

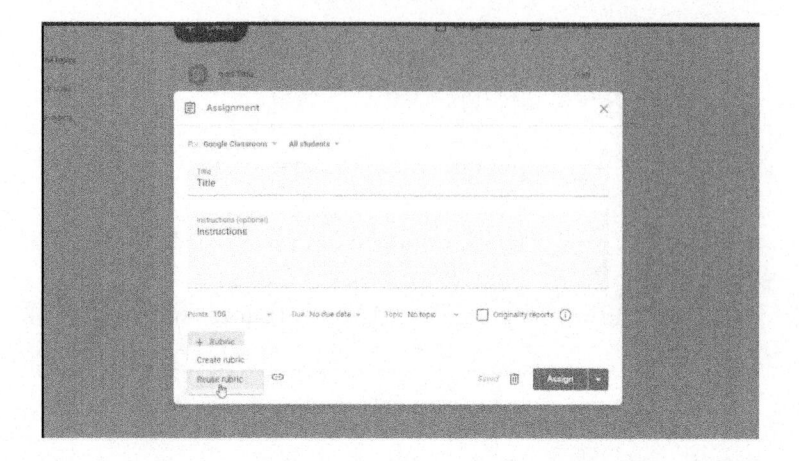

- Enter "Select Rubric" and click on the title. You can select Rubric from a different class by entering the class name OR by clicking the drawdown and select the Class.

- View or Edit rubric, click on "preview," click on "Select and Edit" to edit, save changes when it's done. Go back and click "Select to view."

View Rubric Assignments

- Click on "Rubric."

- Click the arrow up down icon for Expand criteria.

- Click the arrow down up icon for Collapse criteria.

The grading rubric can be done from the Student work page or the grading tool.

Sharing a Rubric

This is possible through export. The teacher creates the Rubric exports, and these are saved to a class Drive called Rubric Exports. This folder can be shared with other teachers and imported into their Assignment.

The imported Rubric can be edited by the teacher in their Assignment, and this editing should not be carried out in the Rubric Exports folder.

Export

- Click on "Rubric."

- Click "More" on the top-right corner and enter "Export to Sheets."

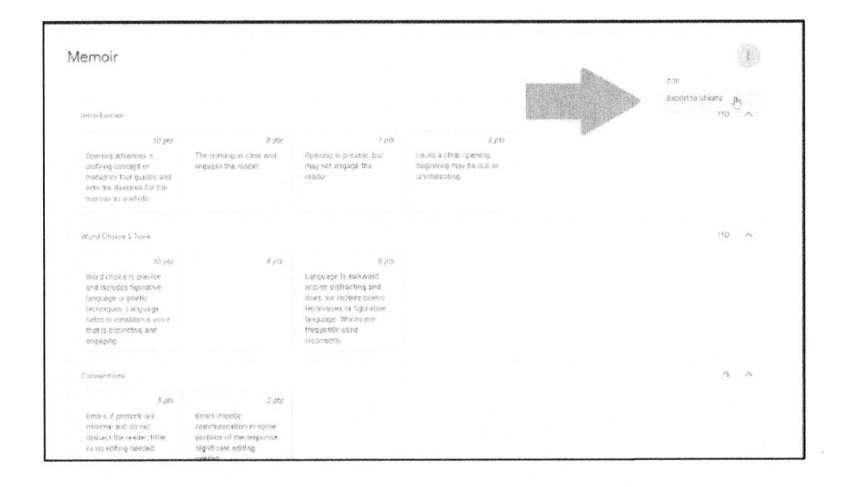

- Return to Classwork page by clicking close (cross sign) at the top-left corner.

- At the top of the Classwork page, click on Drive folder and enter My Drive.

- Select an option, to share one rubric, right-click the "Rubric." To share a rubric folder, right-click on the folder.

- After right-clicking, click on Share and input the e-mail you are sharing to.

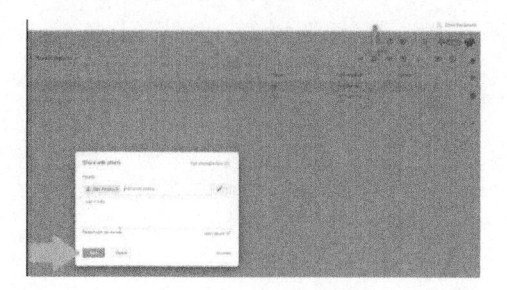

- Then click "Send."

Editing Rubric Assignment

- Click on the "Rubric."

- Click on "More" at the top-right corner and enter "Edit."

- Click "Save" after making changes.

Deleting Rubric Assignment

- Click on "Rubric."

- Click on "More" at the top-right corner and enter "Delete."

- Click "Delete" to confirm.

Posting, Scheduling, or Saving Draft Assignment

Post

- Open Classwork and click on Assignment.

- Click on the drawdown beside Assign, on the top-right corner.

- Click on Assign to post the "Assignment."

Schedule

- Click on the drawdown beside "Assign," on the top-right corner

- Enter "Schedule."

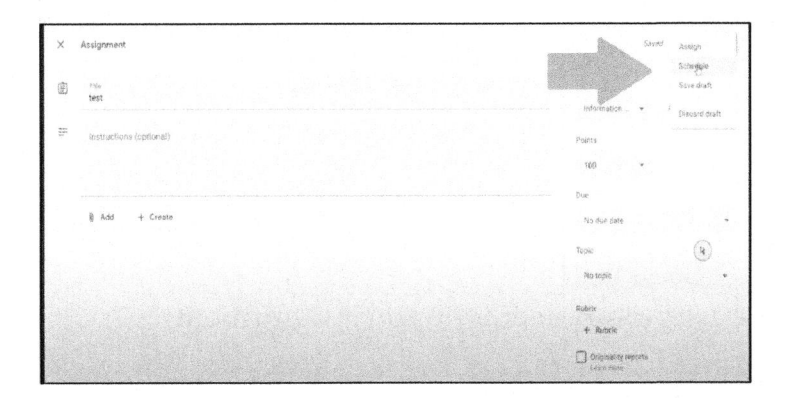

- Input and the date you want the "Assignment" posted.

- Click "Schedule."

Save

- Click on the drawdown beside Assign, on the top-right corner.

- Enter "Save Draft."

- Editing "Assignment:"

- Open "Classwork."

- Click on "More" (three-dot) close to "Assignment:" and enter "Edit."

pag. 172

- Input the changes and save for posted or schedule "Assignment," while Go to Save draft, to save the draft assignment.

Adding Comments to Assignment

- Open "Classwork."

- Click "Assignment" and Enter "View Assignment."

- Click on "Instructions at the top."

- Click on "Add Class Comment."

- Input your comment and Post.

To Reuse Announcement and Assignment

Announcement

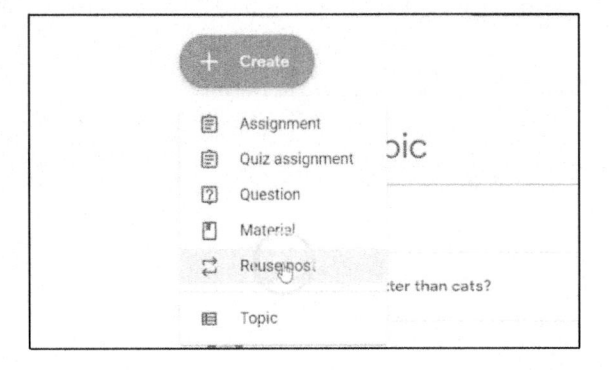

- Open the Class.

- Select "Stream."

- Slide into the Share something with your class box and click on a square clockwise up and down arrow or "Reuse" post.

Assignment

- Open "Classwork" and click on "Create."

- Click on a square clockwise up and down arrow or "Reuse" post.

- Select the "Class and Post" you want to reuse.

- Then click on "Reuse."

Delete an Assignment

- Open "Classwork."

- Click on More (three-dot) close to "Assignment."

- Click on "Delete" and confirm it.

Creating a Quiz Assignment

- Open "Classwork" and click on "Create."

- Click "Quiz Assignment."

- Input the title and instructions.

- You can switch on Locked mode on Chromebooks to ensure the student can't view other pages when taking the quiz.

- You can switch on "Grade Importing" to import grades.

Response and Return of Grades

Response

- Open "Classwork."

- Click on "Quiz Assignment" and free "Quiz Attachment."

- Click on "Edit" and input "Response."

Return

- Open "Classwork."

- Click on "Quiz Assignment."

- Pick the student and click on "Return."

- Confirm "Return."

CHAPTER 9:

Difference between Google Classroom and other Platforms

Let's talk about Google Classroom versus Apple Classroom. Google Classroom is the focus of this book, but how does it stack up to Apple Classroom? Well, read on to find out.

The Hardware Differences

The biggest difference that you'll run into is the hardware elements. Apple Classroom is free for iPad, and the classroom involves using multiple different iPads, and the teachers will put these on the device, allowing students to use them as an integrative tool.

The teacher iPad is a collection of these powers, in order to give a learning experience.

Essentially, it's similar to Google Classroom, and once it is configured; it's connected to devices and the iPad is shared.

Then once the session is done, it can be signed out of. It's a way to keep students focused, shows students different screens, and it can share documents with the class through the use of AirDrop. It shows student work on Apple TV, resets the passwords for students, creates groups of students based on the apps they use, and allows teachers to create groups and teams.

Basically, it's a way to have Apple within the classroom, and through the use of the iPad; it's more collaborative directly within the direct learning atmosphere.

Good for Lower Level Grades

Now you'll notice immediately that the only similarity is that they both include the word "classroom." This means that Apple Classroom is more of a direct classroom tool, and it helps teachers show apps and pages to students who might have trouble with them, and shows off the work that's there. Teachers in upper grades benefit from this because it monitors the activity, but the thing is, students can find out if the teacher is watching very quickly. It's more of a direct device to use for learning within the classroom, whereas with Google Classroom, focuses on both in and outside the classroom.

Google Classroom Focuses on Organization

One big part of Google Classroom is the organization element. It is all collaborated with Google drive, which means that learning is based on connections and education is based on the organization rather than directly in a physical classroom. Google Classroom makes it easy for teachers to assign the work and allows students to have better organization for assignments. It also allows them to get updates faster. You get the opportunity to go paperless too, which is a big plus. Google Classroom focuses on showing work that needs to be done, any grades they have, and any assignments that they missed. It's more of a tool for better organization of the student body over everything else.

Apple Classroom Has More Interactive Lessons

For those teachers who want to have a more engaging class, that's where Apple Classroom may work better. For example, if you're teaching a younger crowd, it may be better to have Apple Classroom because let's face it, do first graders really need to navigate Google drive and submit documents? Course not. They would benefit more from Apple Classroom, since it involves showing the app, and allows teachers to teach and students to focus on what the teacher is teaching. It's focused as well on interacting with the student, and it shows the assignment that they work on; giving teachers a chance to look at each of the pieces of work that the student does, and the most recently used options. There even the screen view that shows the iPad, and it is a good way to keep the direct focus of the students within the classroom.

So, if you're a more interactive-lesson focused teacher, such as you're teaching students the colors, or want students to not screw around in class; the Apple Classroom device may be a better option for you. If you're a teacher who is more interested in having essays, homework, and other elements easily organized in one place, then yes, Google Classroom may be more your style.

Google Classroom Allows For Multiple Devices to Be Used

It is possible to get tablets for Google Classroom, but if you want to have students work on something right away; they totally can. The beauty of Google Classroom is that it's not attached to a brand. You can get Google on your computers and installing chrome is super easy. With that, you are given way more options on using it. Google Classroom can be downloaded as an app too on your device, meaning that if you've got a phone, tablet, or whatever; you're essentially free to use it with whatever you want. That's what's so nice about it, because students can work on assignments right away, and from there, submit it to the teacher. It is also possible for students to work on different subjects while on the go and they can share different questions and resources with the teacher. This is much more interactive, and is perfect for a classroom with multiple smart devices.

The problem with Apple is that it's a brand. You are essentially working only with the Apple brand, meaning that it's highly limited. After all, not everyone may have a Mac or an iPad, so it doesn't really have as much use as say, Google Classroom does.

You Don't Have To Choose

The reality of this though, is that there are some key differences, and you can choose based on needs, with Apple classroom being more of a focus directly within the class environment itself, and Google classroom being more on workflow and assignments. They're two different tools, but comparing it is like comparing apples with oranges, which is a bit different from your average device comparison, since they are often pitted against each other in the technology realm. The truth is you shouldn't have to choose between them, because some teachers benefit from both. If you really want to make your classroom the best it can be, sometimes the best answer is to add both of these services, since they're both really good at what they do, and they complement each other well. The answer is you shouldn't choose one or the other. If you want to get both, get both. If the district can handle both, get both. But, if you're a teacher for a younger group of students, Apple Classroom works. If you're a teacher for older students, Google Classroom works.

Apple Classroom and Google Classroom are two very different types of software, but both of them accomplish the goal of helping children learn better, so they can use these skills to better their lives now and in their futures learning endeavors and studies that they will embark on.

CHAPTER 10:

Best Extensions for Both Teachers & Students

The greater part of the advanced student work is done inside an internet browser. On the off chance that you are in school or college, odds are a large portion of your work, and examining is additionally done in the program.

In this segment, I will manage you through the absolute best Chrome extensions each student must-have. A portion of these will assist you with getting progressively gainful; some will assist you with forestalling botches in your composition.

These Google Chrome extensions are allowed to introduce and the applications are excessively simple to utilize.

Grammar & Spelling Tools

Grammarly

Grammarly is a propelled language checking tool that tests your composition against several linguistic mix-ups.

The free form of this application will assist you with forestalling linguistic slip-ups in the vast majority of your composition. Another exceptional thing about this extension is that it chips away at a large number of the sites which incorporate Google Gmail Record, Google Doc, and some more. It can't be contrast with most other sentence structure tools, since it gives the choice for you to choose which English you compose—regardless of whether American or English.

The exceptional variant of this application won't just assist you with checking for language structure botches, however, it will likewise assist you with checking your content against counterfeiting. It additionally causes you to set a pace for your composition and proposes alterations as needs to be.

Language Tool

Language Tool Chrome Extension

Despite the fact that Chrome's worked in spell checker can assist you to fix some spelling botches, it is worked to assist you with checking and fix syntactic mistakes. Language Tool will assist you with comprehending sentence structure mistakes in excess of 20 distinct dialects.

This tool chips away at a few sites both via web-based networking media and furthermore on email inboxes. Language Tool serves to underlines any content that needs adjustment and furthermore permits you to comprehend any syntactic mistake with only a tick. It assists with stamping in content with spelling botches and furthermore fix linguistic mistakes.

Grammarbase

Grammar Base is a free sentence structure checking tool that checks for everything from Accentuation to Style. It can assist you with fixing syntactic mistakes in your composition with only a single tick. It likewise checks your content against literary theft.

The best part about this syntax checker is that it is totally free and doesn't require any moves up to open more highlights. It deals with practically all sites including Gmail and Facebook.

Ginger

Ginger is one of the most well-known syntax checking tools on the Web. It permits you to fix sentence structure botches with only a tick. It likewise causes you to get recommendations for clearness and rethinking sentences.

With this tool, you can without much of a stretch interpret the content with a single tick. With the free form, you can fix practically all basic sentence structure botches in your composition and records over the web. This tool with Reddit, Facebook, Gmail, Google Docs, and practically even some different destinations.

Plagiarism Checkers

Prowritingaid

ProWritingAid is a free tool that checks your composition for sentence structure slip-ups and offers proposals to improve your composing style. It can assist you with forestalling missteps and make your composing more grounded. It additionally accompanies a written falsification checker.

It takes a shot at practically all sites over the web including email inboxes, Twitter, and other famous locales. It accompanies an implicit Thesaurus that offers proposals to improve your composition. All the proposals can be applied with only a single tick directly from the content as this extension will feature the content consequently that needs revision or improvement.

Plagly

Plagly is a language checker and written falsification checker. It checks your content against a huge number of pages on the web and reports stealing entries in your content. It likewise offers proposals to fix language structure mistakes in your composition.

In spite of the fact that the initial hardly any activities are free; you have to pay a moderate month to month expense to get full access to the tool and boundless copyright infringement checking.

Mybib

MyBB is a free reference generator extension for Google Chrome. This chrome extension prompts you on whether a source is believable. It will assist you with generating references dependent on in excess of 9000 upheld, pre-characterized reference styles which incorporates APA, AMA, MLA, Harvard, and Chicago. You can either duplicate your book reference to the clipboard or download it as a Word record. It can do what Easy Bib and Refer to This for Me improve. This is my suggested tool. CITE THIS FOR ME

Cite This for Me naturally makes site references and referencing in reports with a wide range of styles to look over. The styles incorporate Chicago, APA, MLA, and Harvard. It does everything with only a tick of a catch. It permits you to make lovely references that look great and are adequate for scholarly use.

Easybib

Easy Bib is a free Chrome extension that refers to sites with a single tick and it additionally informs you of the validity concerning the sites you are referring to. It is vastly improved to depend on Easy Bib than a theory all alone. It can inform you which references are acceptable and can be utilized and the one you ought to maintain a strategic distance from simply like a plague.

Google Dictionary

Google Dictionary Google's legitimate Chrome extension that permits you to see definitions straightforwardly from Google's authentic word reference. Not anymore looking through words on Google to check their significance or spelling.

You can either tap the chrome extension symbol and type/glue the word you need Google to characterize. Or then again, you can basically double-tap a word anyplace on the page and this extension will show you the significance in a little in-line popup box.

Power Thesaurus

Power Thesaurus is a free Chrome extension that can show you the antonyms and equivalents without leaving the page you found the word on. It can assist you with improving your composition by making it super-simple to discover comparable, all the more remarkable words to supplant your powerless words.

You can check the Thesaurus utilizing this extension by either choosing a word and right-tapping the choice. Or, on the other hand, you can tap the extension symbol in the menu bar to type the word physically and search the Thesaurus.

Quillbot

Quillbot is a free chrome extension that causes you to supplant words with their choices from the Thesaurus with only a tick. Rather than discovering options for each word all alone; you can essentially place a passage or sentence in this tool and snap the Plume it catches to create another section with elective words.

Stay Focused

In the event that you don't care for squandering hours via web-based networking media locales or even YouTube, at that point this application named 'Remain Centered' is the correct chrome extension you have been searching for. It helps square diverting sites by limiting 5-minute online networking registration which can transform into hours.

This extension permits you to set an everyday stipend limit for "internet-based life and diverting sites." It defaults to just 10 minutes. Your day by day remittance is the quantity of minutes you are permitted to peruse the locales in your interruption list.

On the off chance that you are a bad-to-the-bone profitability nerd; you can empower the atomic alternative from the settings which obstruct all the sites totally. The atomic choice can hinder all sites on the off chance that you need to invest energy disconnected dealing with troublesome stuff when you can't manage the cost of interruptions.

In the event that you need to peruse the Web openly on ends of the week or after work; you can modify the Dynamic Hours and Dynamic Days alternatives. You can enter all the locales you wish to obstruct in the interruptions list from the alternatives menu or you can tap the extension's symbol in the menu bar and add the present site to the rundown from that point.

Evernote Web Clipper

Evernote is the most mainstream note-taking application utilized by a large number of individuals around the globe. It can cause you increasingly beneficial as well as helps you to recall all that you learn. The best part about utilizing Evernote is the capacity to catch notes from online content, for example, website pages, messages, and other content with only a tick.

Evernote's note-taking procedure can accelerate your work process and offer a simple method to store all that you learn.

Evernote Web Scissors permits you to catch nearly everything on the Web. From inquire about material to images; you can save everything to your Evernote account with only a couple of snaps.

This extension additionally permits you to take screen captures. The best part about this extension is that it permits you to catch just pieces of a page. In addition, it can assist you with choosing the contents of website pages like Tweets, Reddit Posts, Blog Entries, and some more.

The great part for sparing content with the Internet Scissors is that you have a made sure about duplicate in your Evernote whether the page is on the web or has gone disconnected.

Todoist

Todoist is one of the most famous lineups for the day applications. It offers applications for all gadgets including Android, iOS, and so forth. Keeping a lineup for the day in your mind will just injure your efficiency. The Todoist Chrome extension permits you to remain beneficial the entire day without overlooking any of your assignments. The spotless interface makes it simple to watch out for every one of your undertakings for the afternoon.

Todoist is made in light of coordinated effort. You can without much of a stretch work together with others who use Todoist on the undertakings and ventures. You can leave remarks on assignments for your schoolmates.

What I like the most about Todoist is that it naturally proposes you time and date for undertakings dependent on your calendar. At the point when you make an assignment, it will propose a date on the off chance that you click the calendar symbol close to the undertaking name.

To improve your work process, Todoist permits you to partition your errands with activities and marks. You can likewise make channels to channel errands dependent on needs, undertakings, and what their identity is allotted to. Todoist can be an insignificant plan for the day or an undeniable profitability machine with bunches of highlights, for example, Undertakings, Marks, Rehash, Updates, Channels, Names, and some more.

Dualless

Dualless encourages you to work with two open windows one next to the other. Taking a shot at only one screen can be tiring a direct result of all the exchanging between different windows. On the off chance that you can't manage the cost of two screens; you can utilize Dualless to mastermind two windows next to each other with only a couple of snaps.

You can relocate windows next to each other yourself however this extension encourages you to do it with only a couple of snaps. Dualless offers a wide range of design varieties to browse. You should simply choose two tabs you need to part and snap the extension's symbol to choose the window split design.

CHAPTER 11:

Tips and Tricks

Both teachers and students can benefit from Google Classroom. It is a secure platform that brings together some of the best apps that Google has to offer to help teachers get the most out of their lectures and students to learn in new and exciting ways. Here we will look at some of the tips and tricks that both students and teachers can try to get the most out of the Google Classroom platform.

Tips for Teachers

Tip 1: Learn all the ways to give feedback.

Your students are going to thrive with as much feedback as you can provide them, and the classroom offers you many options for this. You can leave comments on assignments that students hand in, on the file that is submitted, through email, and so much more. Consider the best places to leave feedback and let your students know so they can be on the lookout for ways to improve.

Some of the ways that you can utilize comments include:

- **Class comments**—you can do this by starting a common for the whole class on the outside of the assignment or in the announcement. It is going to be a comment that the entire course is going to see, so don't use it if you just want to talk to the individual student. It is an excellent option to use if you're going to answer a question that a lot of people have.

- **Private comments**—you can do this by going into the file of an individual student. You will be able to see the submissions this student has made and can click on the comment bar near the bottom. When you add a comment, the student will be the only one who can see it.

- **Comments to media**—you can do this by clicking on the file that the student submitted to you. Highlight the area and then comment on that particular part of the project. It can help you to show an example of the student or explain your thoughts and how something needs to be changed.

Tip 2: Use the description feature

When creating an assignment, make sure to add a nice long description. It is where you explain what the task is all about, how to complete it, and even when the assignment is due. Often students are juggling many classes all at once, and by the time they get to the task; they have forgotten all the instructions you gave them in class. Or if a student missed class that day; the description can help them understand what they missed. A good report can help to limit emails with questions and can help students get started on the assignment without confusion.

Tip 3: Reuse some of your old posts

At times, you may have an assignment, question, or announcement that is similar to something you have posted before. For example, if you have a weekly reading or assess task that is pretty much the same every week; you will be able to use the reuse option in the classroom. To do this, just click on the "+" button that is on the bottom right of the screen, and then you will then be able to select "Reuse post." Pick from a list of options that you already used for the class. If there are any modifications, such as a different due date, you can make those before posting again. When reusing the post, you have the option to create new copies of the attachments that were used in the original posting.

Tip 4: Share your links and resources

There may be times that you find a fascinating document, video, or other media that you would like your students to see. Or, they may need resources for an upcoming project, and you want to make it easier for them to find. In this case, you should use the announcement feature. It allows all the essential documents to be listed right at the top of the classroom rather than potentially getting lost further down in assignments.

It is a great tip to use for items of interest that you would like to share with your students or for documents and files that they will need right away. If you have a resource that the students will need throughout the year; you should place it into the "About" tab to prevent it from getting lost as the year goes on.

Tips for Students

Tip 1: Pick one email for all of your classes

Consider having a dedicated email that is for all of your classes. You don't need to separate it and have an email for each of your categories, but create a new email that will only accept information from all classes using Google Classroom. Whenever a teacher announces they use this platform; you will use this email. It helps you to keep all of your courses in one place and can prevent you from missing out on your announcements and assignments because they got lost in all your emails.

Tip 2: Check your classes daily

As the year goes on, your teacher will probably get into a routine of when they make posts and you can check the class at that time. But it is still a good idea to stay on top of a class and check it each day. You never know when you may forget about an assignment that is almost due or when the teacher will add a special announcement for the whole class. If you only check your levels on occasion; you could miss out on a lot of valuable information along the way. Check-in daily to stay up to date and to get everything in on time.

Tip 3: Look at the Calendar

One of the first places you should go when opening up to a class is the calendar. It is going to list everything necessary that is coming your way in the few months (updated as the teacher adds new announcements and assignments), so you can plan out your time. For some students, it is easier to get a grasp on the work when it is in tablet form rather than just looking at a date in the announcements. Use this as a planning tool and check it often to see if there is anything new to add to your schedule.

Tip 4: Ask questions for clarification

The classroom makes it easier for students to ask the questions they need before starting an assignment. In some classes, it can be hard to find time to ask a question. When twenty or more students are asking questions at the same time, or the teacher runs out of time and barely gets the assignment out before the bell, many students may leave the classroom without any clue how to begin on a task.

With the classroom, the students can ask any questions they have when it is convenient. If they have a question about an assignment; they can comment on the task or send an email.

If they have a question about some feedback that is left for a test or essay; they can ask it right on the assignment.

The classroom has opened up many options for talking to your teacher and getting your questions answered, so don't be shy and sit in the dark when you need clarification.

Tip 5: Learn about all the features of Google

Google has many great features that both students and teachers can take advantage, many people don't realize all of the different apps that are available on Google, and since these apps can be used together with the classroom and are free, it is essential to take advantage of as many as possible. Some of the best Google products that can help with learning include:

- **Gmail**—Gmail makes it easier for students and teachers to communicate about the class without sharing the information with other students.

- **Calendar**—students will be able to see at a glance when essential assignments, tests, and additional information occur in their class.

- **Drive**—Drive is a great place to put all tasks, questions, and other documents that are needed to keep up in class. Teachers can place learning materials and assignments inside for the student to see, and students can submit their jobs all in one place.

- **YouTube**—students are used to spending time on YouTube, and teachers can use this to their advantage to find educational videos for their class. Students can either look at links that the teacher provides or search for their videos.

- **Docs**—this program works similarly to Microsoft Word, but since it is free, it can be helpful for those students who don't already have Word at home. Students can write, edit, and make changes just like on regular documents and then submit them back to the teacher.

- **Google Earth/Maps**—explores the world around us with these two great features. Google Earth lets students learn more about the world by allowing them to look up different areas and see them from an actual satellite. Google Maps can help with Geography around the world, or students can even create their Maps with this program.

These are just a few of the different apps available with Google that can make a difference in the way that students learn. While not all of them will apply to every class, a good understanding of each can help the teacher pick the right one for their quality and helps the student learn as much as possible.

Tip 6: Don't forget about tests and quizzes

Sometimes, a teacher may give you a few days to complete a test at home if there isn't enough time to do everything in the classroom. It gives you a bit of freedom to study for longer and fit the test around your schedule, but when a check isn't due right away; it is sometimes easy to forget about it. Make sure to watch your calendar and set up announcements to remind yourself that a vital assignment or test is due.

The issue with forgetting about some of these things is that with the right add-ons, the system may grade the test as incomplete or give you zero (if the test is multiple choices). The teacher may be willing to go back in and fix the grade or extend the due date if you talk to them, but it is still better to just get the test done in the first place. It shows that you can adhere to deadlines and saves some time for your teacher.

Google Classroom may seem like a simple platform, but there is just so much that you can do with it both as a teacher and as a student. The options for learning, sending information back and forth, and all the organization and freedom now available in the classroom can make this an attractive choice for many schools.

CHAPTER 12:

FAQs about Google Classroom

As a teacher, there are a lot of different options that you can use to make the most out of your classroom and you may be curious as to why Google Classroom is the best option to help you out. There are many questions that you may have that pertain to Google Classroom. Some of the questions that you may have about Google Classroom include:

Is It Easy to Get Started with Google Classroom?

Yes, it is really easy to work with Google Classroom, but you do need to remember that it is necessary to have the Google Apps for Education and your domain needs to be verified.

How Are Apps for Education and Classroom Connected?

To keep things simple, Google Classroom is not able to work without the help of Google Apps for Education. While you are able to use the Apps for Education all on its own; you will find that using Google Classroom is going to help to make all of it organized and it is much easier to work with. With the help of both the Classroom and Apps working together, both the students and the teachers are able to access the spreadsheets, slideshows, and documents as well as other links without having to worry about attachments and more. Even giving and receiving assignments and grades are easier when these two are combined together. In addition, there is the option to download the Classroom Mobile app, which will make it easier to access your classes whenever and wherever you would like. This is going to be great for students who are on the go and don't have time to always look through their laptop to see announcements. Even teachers are able to use this mobile app to help them get up assignments and announcements when they are on the go so, they can concentrate on other tasks later on.

Does It Cost to Use Google Classroom?

One of the best things about using Google Classroom is that it is completely free. All you need is a bit of time to help get it all set up, but it will not include any out of pocket costs to make it work. You will have to wait about two weeks in the beginning for your application to be reviewed before you are able to use the class, so consider setting this up early to prevent issues with falling behind. You will never have to pay for anything when you are using Google Classroom. If you run into a vendor who is asking for you to pay for Google Classroom; you should report them to Google. It is highly likely that this is a fake vendor so do not work with them or provide them with any of your payment information. Google Classroom is, and always will be, free for you to use.

Can I Still Use Classroom If It Is Disabled on My Domain?

One of the nice things about working with Classroom is that even if it has been disabled on a certain domain, you are still able to use it. With that being said, there are going to be a few restrictions. While you may still be able to get access to a lot of the features, such as Google Drive, Google Docs, and Gmail; you may not be able to see some of the slides, docs, and sheets that were saved in the classroom. It is always best to have your domain turned on when you are working in Google Classroom because this ensures that you are able to use all of the features that are available through the Classroom.

Do I Need to Have Gmail Enabled to Use Classroom?

It is not necessary to have Gmail enabled in order to use the Google Classroom. You are able to use the Classroom as much as you would like without enabling Gmail, but you would find that you wouldn't be able to receive notifications if the Gmail account isn't turned on. If you would like to have some notifications sent to you, you need to have Gmail enabled. If you are not that fond of using the Gmail account for this; it is possible to set up your own email server to make it work. This way, you will still be able to receive the notifications that are needed from the Classroom while using the email server that you like the most.

Will I Have to Work with Ads on Google Classroom?

Many people like to work with Google Classroom because they don't have to worry about seeing ads all over the place. The classroom was designed for educational purposes, and Google recognizes that people don't want to have to fight with ads all of the time when they are learning. You can rest assured that Google and Classroom are not going to take your information and use it for advertising. This is part of the privacy and security that is offered with Google Classroom, which will protect both the student and the teacher from any phishing or spam.

Yes, those with disabilities are able to use Google Classroom. Some of the features are not yet complete, but Google is working to make some improvements to the classroom so that those who have disabilities can use it too. Aside from using the Screen reader; there are a few other features that you can use with android including:

- **Braille Back:** this is a great feature that is going to allow for Braille to be displayed on the Android Device, as long as you have your Bluetooth installed. This is also going to work with the Screen Reader feature that we talked about before. With this feature, you will also be able to input your text while interacting with your Android device.

- **Switch Access:** it is also possible for you to use Switch Access, which is a tool that allows you to control your device with two or more switches. This is great for those who are dealing with limited mobility. It is also a good way to get notifications and alerts.

You are also able to tweak some of the settings that are in Google Classroom in regards to color correction, magnification, captions, touch and hold, using a speaking password, and more.

As you can see, there are a lot of neat things that you are able to do when it comes to using Google Classroom and it is pretty easy for everyone to be able to use. If you ever have some other questions about Google Classroom; you can always contact their support to get the assistance that you need.

CHAPTER 13:

Pros & Cons of Using Google Classroom

Pros

This platform has several features. Some are shown below:

- **Easy to use:** very easy to use. As M. Janzen said, "Google's classroom program is just a deliberate learning interface and options used to initiate and monitor activities; emails, notifications of relevance to the whole course or person, and gives notices of support."

- **Cloud-based:** Google Classroom offers increasingly sophisticated and valid innovations in the learning environment and Google applications are a series of important cloud-based business communication tools used by all professional staff.

- **Free:** there are no usage costs. Anyone with or without a Google Account can create and participate in lessons.

- **Compatible with mobile phones:** as M. Janzen said, "Today's educational environment requires access to interesting and simple study materials." Google Classroom is designed to be responsive. Useful for use on any cell phone.

- **Save time:** Google Classroom saves students and teachers time. As Iftekhar said, "Coordinating with other Google

pag. 198

applications such as presentations, documents, records, and spreadsheets. The whole process of evaluation, activities, reviews, formative evaluations, and feedback is divided and simplified."

Cons

Despite its many benefits, Google Classroom is limited. Such as:

- **Limited options:** Google Classroom is not synchronized with Google Calendar or other calendars. It is difficult for teachers to prescribe curricula and set deadlines for assignments.

- **About "goggles:"** Pappas describes Google Classroom as "goggles." This includes some buttons known to Google customers. In this case, people who see customers of Google articles for the first time (such as elementary and college students) can be confused or do more to learn these signs. Only Google Classroom coordinates YouTube to share videos. Other popular tools like SlideShare, Facebook, and others don't work in Google Classroom.

- **No mechanical updates:** Google Classroom does not automatically receive updates of streaming activities. Students must have the usual prerequisites, otherwise, clear notice is required.

- **Difficult to share with students:** it is not possible to share files with many classmates unless students become file owners. However, if you become the owner of the file, you must ask the teacher for permission to share the archive.

- **Change the problem:** after creating and distributing the project, students become owners of the archive. As owners, they have the right to change. In the long run, if desired, all parts of the project can be revoked, even if by chance by some students.

- **There are no automatic tests and quizzes:** Google Classroom does not compile computer-related exams and tests. Therefore, it cannot replace the other available learning management systems (LMS).

- **Impersonal:** still provides a mixed resume but is not compatible with other instant messenger programs such as Google Hangouts. In this case, Google Docs makes collaboration between students and teachers difficult. Basically, live chat is unlikely in Google Classroom; at least not yet.

Google Classification Teaching Quality

To monitor that Google Classroom affects listening skills; experts analyze the following search opportunities for research and make some recommendations.

This research is an operational research conducted by 40 scholars from Daffodil International University in Bangladesh. The Master is a first-year student with a degree in ordinary English. Scientists use quantitative research methods to gather information. The statistical analysis of relative percentages and student achievement levels was obtained from four different projects that had an impact on student skills. Experts found a lot of help from hearaminute.com in building search tools. This research was conducted with the permission of the university authorities.

To complete this study, Google Classroom researchers created a classroom called "Student Skills" and invited students to participate. Since students use Gmail accounts for a domain check (provided by the university), they can easily enter the classroom. The experts assigned four listening projects for the presentation for four consecutive weeks. Activities are a basic exercise to fill gaps and correct them together.

ELT experts point out that "listening skills" are one of the four language skills that are ignored, as they lack the ability and training to make positive use of the resources available to teach listening L2 students. This is conceived by students and teachers.

Students in Bangladesh tend to develop their English learning experience. However, today's young people are familiar with technology, which is an integrated resource for ELT professionals conducting research. This shows how Google Classroom can be used as a learning tool to improve students' listening skills. As a result, the positive impact of using Google Classroom on college lenders proves its worth.

Conclusion

Finally, the doubt on whether you are a beginner on Google Classroom is disappeared currently. The reality is that also the so-called "pro" would certainly doff their hats for you if you are able to sensibly make use of the text succinctly. If you doubt that, then find among them and exchange expertise and also see his/her comment on you. You have been taught on the benefits of Google Classroom, which undoubtedly was the first thing you learnt. The advantage is inexhaustible yet the significant ones are embedded below and also you can flaunt it is not a wild-goose chase to take on the use of Google Classroom.

Yet, you found out about just how to get going with Google Classroom, which is very important. Many stuck at the astonishing stage of concept regarding numerous inventions or technology or service since they lack understanding exactly how to get it began. You discovered the site link and also requires you require to keep the setting when starting using Google Classroom. Really it is a crucial aspect of it however not the main due to the fact that without more activities and knowledge concerning another other, you are like not beginning it.

After registration as well as being part of the elite neighborhood of teachers or trainees who await the future; you still relocated further to discover how to utilize Google Classroom. The action is necessary as you were shown on how to produce class, just how to structure it, how students can join your class, how to welcome therefore several others. These are crucial details you require to get familiarized with due to the fact that you will certainly use them each day you are instructing.

Likewise, applications that can be used in simplifying your ease of access and also for benefit were taught. There are a large number of applications with their unique attributes and contents that make making use of Google Classroom better on different tools. Some of the applications that were highlighted and also clarified are BookWidget, Duncee, Nearpod, and so on. These applications with various other good one's support using Google Classroom on your device at your convenient time. More so, student approach ideas were educated in the body of the text after the intro of the applications that can be utilized. These ideas are germane to efficient teaching on Google Classroom. You were taught how to email students whatever you want them to understand, how to make the statement, how to make use of the ideal comment you would give class, and more.

Making use of Google Classroom can be less complicated by adopting the best practices and methods for the tasks you want to carry out. Various best practices and also techniques were intimated to you in the body of the text. These were instructed to get the most out of the classroom, so you must endeavor to use it continually. Additionally, the functions offered on Google Classroom as well as devices that can be beneficially used. There are numerous features such as Assignments, Notifications, Comments, Google Forms, Google Schedule, etc. that you may be oblivion of unless you are taught. They make Google Classroom more interesting as they create an avenue for simpler teaching and learning at the same time. They collectively beautify the learning setting for both the teachers and the students. Detailed procedures of using them were found out in this text.

Using Google Classroom can be easier when the nitty-gritty of how to communicate with the trainee successfully is known. Therefore, a thorough description on how to communicate with the student using the Google Classroom was offered. The stipulation of that does not just make Google Classroom simpler however likewise streamlines the teaching and also removes the trouble several educators have while teaching in physical class. Afterward, a much more detailed explanation on how to prepare the assignment, grade it as well as announcements were provided to you. On top of that, much like the traditional physical class; you would need to return the task given in order to grade it and record, so a method to accomplish that on Google Classroom was given. The intriguing component is that; all works can be collected from all the students on the same web page.

Making use of modern technology such as the Google Classroom in order to obtain the commitment of trainees was shown. The primary reason behind adopting the brand-new approach and also attempting new things such as the use of Google Classroom is to acquire the academic objective.

The attainment of the objective hinges on the students' commitment, so the demand for it. Nonetheless, ideal practices that can be embraced in the Google Classroom were brought to you. The need for it is clear just as you need a mentor to look forward to in anything you intend to do well.

Lastly, how to improve your teaching by making use of Google Classroom was discovered. There are various methods to do that, some of the instructed ones are using partnership/collaboration, keeping tab of activities, use of Google calendar judiciously, integrating of Google Forms, Google Drive, Google Sites, Google Maps, and various other services such as YouTube within the Google Classroom.

Now I believed you must have been attempting everything you found out until now on Google Classroom, nevertheless, if you have not, why not start now. Now that you have all the tools required, take your tool, and also start using them.

ZOOM FOR TEACHERS STEP BY STEP GUIDE

A BEGINNER'S GUIDE TO ZOOM 2020 – 2021.
SCREENSHOTS, TIPS, AND TRICKS TO BECOME THE BEST MODERN TEACHER.

RICHARD V. ROSS

Introduction

Zoom Video Communications is an independent information service located in California. It provides video telecommunications and online messaging services through a peer-to-peer software system based in the cloud. It is used for video conferencing, working from home, distance learning, and social connections. Zoom's corporate model relies on delivering a product that is easier to use than alternatives, as well as cost advantages, which involves reducing infrastructure-level hardware expenses and ensuring a strong degree of workforce productivity. It supports a video chatting service, which allows unlimited access to up to a hundred devices at once, with a time limit of forty minutes for free accounts having meetings with five or more members.

Customers have the opportunity to update by subscription to one of their plans, with the maximum allowing up to a thousand persons simultaneously, with no time limit. With the emergence of remote working in this scenario, Zoom's software utilization has seen a significant global rise starting in early 2020. Its software applications have been subject to review by the public and media concerning privacy and security issues. A portion of the Zoom working population is based in China that has given rise to concerns about monitoring and censorship.

Business conferencing apps such as Zoom Rooms are accessible for fifty to one hundred dollars a month. One screen can display up to forty-nine users at once. Zoom has several levels: Basic, Pro, Enterprise, and Business. If you are using Mozilla Firefox or Google Chrome, participants do not have to download the app; they can click on the link and enter from the web page. For Macs, Zoom is not compatible with Safari.

Banking institutions, universities, and other educational departments around the globe use Zoom. Zoom has a record of ten million regular customers, and the app had more than two hundred million active users in March 2020, generating expanded difficulties for the business. The company launched version 5.0 of Zoom in April which resolved a range of privacy and security issues. It includes the default passwords, enhanced authentication, and a meeting place security icon.

You can work remotely on your passion with video conferencing through Zoom. Zoom has features that can help you to organize a meeting formally. Zoom is the best tool for online teaching as it gives whiteboard, annotation, screen sharing, keyboard shortcuts, and much more. Scheduling, joining, starting a conference, and sending invitations to your participants for a video conference is easy with Zoom. It has an assignment and presentations set up as a tool for instructors to involve students in a better learning process. For feedback, there is a polling feature to create a poll and share it with your participants. If you are looking for an application for your meetings and video/audio conferences, try out Zoom as it will provide you with the best features as compared to other tools, including price plans.

Zoom is a simple program that is fun and intuitive to use, yet it holds such a wide array of features that many may slip beneath your notice. This book aims to explain the vast majority of these features to you as they are, at the time writing, from the perspective of a current and active user. If Zoom's user manuals feel too daunting, too technical, or too impersonal, here you will find simple, easy-to-understand step-by-step guides that'll walk you through everything you'll need to know. Before explaining how to install and use the software, however, let us first go over why you should use Zoom software and services. It is recommended that you begin working with Zoom as soon as possible; we live in an ever-innovative world, where technology is constantly changing and adapting. The sooner you learn this knowledge, the better the foundation you can lay for yourself with the information within.

CHAPTER 1:

Introduction To Zoom Cloud Meeting

What is zoom?

Zoom is an online conferencing application with a central, desktop interface and a smartphone device for users to communicate from any place, with on or off video. Users may decide to record meetings, work on activities, and view or edit on screens with each other, all in one easy-to-use application. Zoom offers high -quality video, audio, and remote screen networking functionality through Windows Phone, Mac devices, iOS, Android, Blackberry, Zoom, and H.322/SIP room networks. Zoom is typical all along and commonly used in this scenario. The video conferencing system has

pag. 210

been the unquestioned pioneer in space throughout the nine years since its establishment.

Zoom is one of the top video conferencing technology systems worldwide in 2020. It helps you to communicate with fellow workers remotely when in-person interactions are not feasible and have become immensely useful for social activities, too. Zoom has been an essential resource for tiny, medium, and broad teams that want to stay in contact and maintain their normal business processes with limited interruption- as as well as being a firm favorite of users.

Yet due to the current scenario, Zoom has lately seen an increase in technical expertise. When more and more people are being driven to work from home and remain safe, Zoom helps them to participate in fun ways to communicate with their peers. Zoom is useful to companies, with the best features the app provides, three options to Zoom, and much more. If you operate a remote squad, Zoom can help you keep in contact with them through its intuitive features of video conferencing.

There is an expense to using the updated function plans from Zoom. When you have the money, invest in an updated package of Zoom. If the response is no, go back to working with your colleagues just the way you are working in free mode.

As a teacher, if you or your learners have a situation that keeps you from meeting the person, Zoom can help keep your class going. Online class meetings, in which everyone is planning to join a Zoom meeting, are one way to create interaction when learners are remote, but Zoom can also be used to assist other learning and teaching situations. So long as a student attendant is on a laptop, they can select a connection to the URL and be taken to a chat with the instructor instantly. This removes slow updates entirely, annoying bonus services, and plenty of boring things. Often people need to upgrade their software or flash player to connect, but that never transforms into an issue that lasts more than two minutes. It is suitable for first-time gatherings and already-off meetings. Zoom provides different beneficial features for online classes like a whiteboard, screen sharing, screen recording, assignment and presentation setup, etc.

How does zoom work?

Zoom enables one-on-one discussion time that can grow into group calls, vocations, training workshops and websites for internal and external audiences, and international video conferences with up to 1,000 participants and up to 49 screen videos. Freebies allow unlimited meetings one by one but limit group time to 40 minutes and 100 participants. The paid plan starts at $ 15 per month per host.

Zoom plans

For the vast majority of users, the free version of Zoom is sufficient. Even if you plan on hosting a meeting of more than three people for longer than forty minutes, a great and comfortable way to work around the free version of Zoom's time limit is to allow a short 5-15 minute break after your first forty minutes expire, and then simply start a new meeting on the same topic thereafter, as you'll find that nothing is preventing you from doing so.

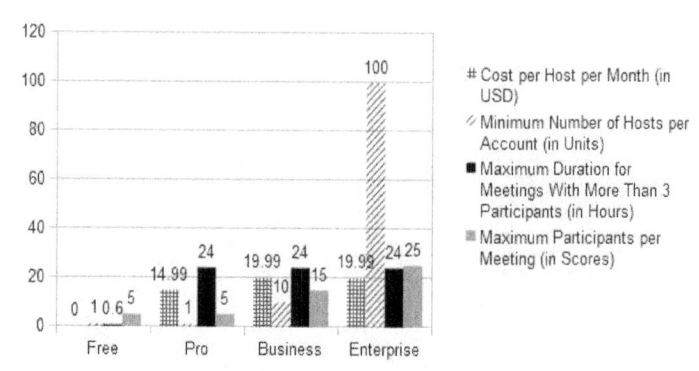

Zoom Account Plans Comparison

Plan	Cost per Host per Month (in USD)	Minimum Number of Hosts per Account (in Units)	Maximum Duration for Meetings With More Than 3 Participants (in Hours)	Maximum Participants per Meeting (in Scores)
Free	0	1	0	6
Pro	14.99	1	24	5
Business	19.99	10	24	15
Enterprise	19.99	50	24	25

Teachers, students, and entrepreneurs in their early stages can likely get by happily on the free version of Zoom with little trouble.

However, there are another three tiers to be aware of, just in case, they'd be better for your specific situation; *Pro*, *Business*, and *Enterprise*. Pricing plans can be found on Zoom's pricing page.

Pro is sufficient for groups and organizations that have a fairly small number of leaders or managers; for instance, a high school might only have nine teachers assigned to its senior grades, and a local business might have a similarly sized managerial staff. In addition to having all the free version's features, Pro also allows meetings to run up to 24 hours at a time; far longer than most would ever consider holding a meeting outside of Congress. Additionally, you, as a host, are provided 1 GB of storage on Zoom's cloud, making it easier to record and distribute your meetings after the end (as if that wasn't easy enough before). You also have the option to host up to 1,000 participants and gain greater cloud storage space if you're willing to pay a little extra for add-ons. Finally, this is the tier where Zoom's Webinar feature becomes available, and you begin gaining specialized admin tools that let you delegate limited host powers to select non-host participants.

This makes Pro an excellent choice over the free version if you need to reinforce a more serious atmosphere, have long talks with large groups of associates without interruptions, or otherwise, wish to ensure conferences remain orderly through empowered delegation of responsibility.

Business, meanwhile, has all the free and Pro features gives you dedicated customer support (meaning response will be faster and more sensitive to your issues), as well as the ability to weave the brand of your company into the meeting, such as with custom URLs, meeting pages and invitation formats. It requires ten hosts at a minimum, however, each of which will need to pay the monthly subscription, meaning this option is best for large, wealthy organizations who have already established themselves in their field. This is a great option for larger organizations who need a competitive edge, more complex administrative hierarchies during meetings, or a stronger professional image during said meetings through branding.

The *Enterprise* tier, however, should only be considered by extremely large multinational corporations with strong international interest and investment due to its high cost and host requirements. Enterprise's biggest advantage over Business is the sheer size of participants it can host (although similar amounts can be hosted cheaper on lower tiers through add-ons), as well as limitless cloud storage and discounts on Webinar and Zoom Room add-ons, which could end up saving money for exceptionally large businesses if they rely on hosting seminars for hundreds or even thousands of people at a time; although for most organizations, this won't be the case.

Difference between free zoom and paid zoom

There are a couple of differences between the free and compensated Zoom Noting.

Free Consumers

You can download the Zoom program onto the telephone or your computer and join any assembly using a meeting ID that is furnished. You may opt to disable video or sound before linking. You might make your free Zoom accounts, such as by connecting your Google account, and from there, you can make a meeting, schedule you, combine a meeting, discuss a display, add contacts, etc. Bear in mind you may only be signed into Zoom on one tablet, a single computer, and a single telephone. Zoom has stated that you'll be logged out on the apparatus while logged in to a different device of the same kind if you register into a device.

Paid Users

You can register and download Zoom on your computer if your system administrator has an Enterprise account, company, or even a Guru, your job email. You need to sync Zoom into your calendar so you can program Zoom meetings and encourage participants that are distant to combine. You're going to require a pc and operate a tablet for attendees along with Zoom Meetings to start the Zoom Meetings if you are establishing a Zoom Room. You will also require a mic, camera, speaker, a minimum of one HDTV screens to show remote meeting participants, along with an HDMI cable to discuss monitors on a screen, in addition to an online cable to your link, you will also have to get "Zoom Rooms for Conference Room" on the in-room pc and "Zoom Room Controller" to your tablet at the assembly area. So workers can see which assembly rooms are accessible and you may then sync these rooms into the shared calendar of your company.

Zoom security updates and issues

Just like every other software app, Zoom is one of the best video conferencing apps. With an increase in demand, it is unavoidable to have glitches or concerns which can be avoided. There are several concerns about Zoom, both with guests concerning safety and issues. The business has made many moves to counter such problems and reassure customers about the value of privacy and security. This includes things like eliminating the assembly ID in this call's title bar; if users discuss screenshots online, the assembly is not subjected to misuse.

Security tips.

Be wary of links: Some of the links sent out for one to join a zoom room or meeting might be fraudulent, and when clicked on might expose your computer or mobile phones to malware attack leaking your documents or destroying it fully.

Waiting rooms: It is also advisable to create a waiting room where participants will be before joining the zoom meeting. This minimizes the potential of uninvited participants disrupting your zoom meetings or classes.

Always remember it's been recorded: Try not to do things you would not be proud of and always remember to **either mute or cancel the camera** if you must attend to something else.

Use a work email: I said it earlier on the importance of using a work email instead of a personal one. This is to avoid a leak of any sort in case zoom's network is hacked

Don't fall for fake zoom apps: Very important, because falling for fake zoom apps would mislead you, and you might end up being hacked.

Troubleshooting

There are common problems associated with using zoom. The most common problems and how to fix them are listed below

Another cause could be that people with computers or telephone speakers might be too close to each other or lastly there might be numerous computers with active audio in the same conference room. The solution to either of these situations is to ask the two people that are too close to each other to move apart. Or one of them would be asked to either leave the audio conference or mute his/her audio on their device.

Problems associated with sharing a screen:

Sharing of the screen is one of the important features of the Zoom app and a zoom meeting and it is easy by clicking **Share Screen at the bottom of the window.** If you're planning to share your screen during a call and it is not working, it might be because you lack a strong internet connection. Sharing your screen takes up a lot of bandwidth/frequency range. If you are on a call or in a meeting and your screen refuses to share, **turn off your video by clicking the Stop Video button and try starting the video again.**

Problems with receiving email messages from Zoom:

Another common problem of the zoom app is not being able to receive confirmatory email messages from Zoom during registration or other notification emails. These usually take between 2 - 30 minutes to arrive and or longer, but if it doesn't arrive, you need to check your spam folder, or you make sure that your email is configured properly.

Time:

To have more time for your meetings, you can upgrade from the basic plan to other plans.

Zoom bombers?

The rise in prominence of Zoom must direct the ceremony to be mistreated by web trolls and individuals with time on their hands. Some people have been searching down insecure and public Zoom meetings and allowing themselves, then "bombing" others on the telephone with picture videos, porn, and other inappropriate content. We composed a guide, and there are methods in which you can stop this from occurring, such as procuring your requirements, preventing display sharing, and disabling video. The staff behind Zoom is currently making improvements to keep them secure and to fasten your requirements.

How to stop zoom bombs:

The easiest way to avoid getting Zoom bombed is to keep your event private and your invite list small. When creating an event for a large audience, do not share your meeting link directly on social media or multiple platforms.

Default Security Upgrades
Zoom has been upgraded to assist invite users. One of them has become the need for a password as the default option for Zoom meetings. This, together with waiting rooms, ensures that they are allowed in. Another measure is safe and safe.

Zoom Safety Tools
Zoom has made it simple to handle and secure your meetings when they are happening. There is a selection of security tools; now, you can access two or three clicks, such as the capability to lock the assembly as it's begun so that no new people, eliminating participants on the phone, can connect along with disabling chat. To get the Zoom safety tools, you may click on the safety button, which looks in the window once the phone is currently occurring, or hover over a player to interact with them.

Reporting Other Participants
It is now possible to record participants who are not welcome or are causing difficulty. Now you can send a report to managing abuse of the machine, in addition to removing them on the telephone. This can help to interfere with calls and prevent them. To accomplish this, click on the safety button and click on the report.

Meeting Connector Core Concepts
Zoom supplies service or a public. In the hybrid cloud assistance, you deploy assembly communication servers known inside the internal system of your company. While the meetings have been hosted on your cloud in doing this, meeting and user metadata are handled in the cloud.

The Zoom Meeting Connector is done via all assembly traffic such as voice, video, and information sharing. The Zoom Meeting Controller may be deployed onto some other virtualization platform and is packed as an OVF.

Networking Schema
The Meeting Connector utilizes the cloud to the Following solutions:

Notification Services for fulfilling invitation notifications on mobile devices and PC

Internet Application Services for meeting and user metadata like login, scheduled assembly list

Cloud Controller for syncing assembly standing
Zoom is an application that you may use to communicate remotely with anyone-either visual or audio-only, or even both when holding live conversations, and it helps you to capture such sessions for playback later. In 2019 over the majority of five hundred companies reportedly used Zoom and hit even higher heights during 2020, claiming three hundred million daily Zoom meeting participants recently.

Zoom is the unquestioned leader in the market when it comes to digital conferencing software. The blend of in-depth functionality, elegant design, and accessible pricing structure allows it a worthy addition to the application framework of every company. Only note to take maximum advantage of all of the services that were provided by Zoom. If you do, you will enjoy all the benefits Zoom has to bring. The program you choose will rely on the team's scale, how much you expect to utilize Zoom, the intent to use the method, and the existing budget.

There were some security issues when the zoom application was launched. With increased demand, the zoom organization takes into account its security issues and updates. The organization has created several movements to counter security issues and reassure users that security and privacy are essential. That involves necessary items like deleting the meeting Identifier from the call's title bar.

The organization has announced multiple changes to the program to improve protection credentials.

News for Meetings and Privacy
Zoom's work continues relentlessly aimed at improving the platform, in particular, the one focused on improving privacy and security. Today on the pages of the official blog two interventions: one on end-to-end encryption which, unlike what was announced at first, will be made available to everyone, the other to report some features that are introduced as part of the 90-Day Security Plan launched in early April. The novelties concern the management of accounts as well as meetings to allow advanced control of what happens during a meeting on Zoom.

Here they are:

Added an option that allows administrators to disable the possibility of authentication through email-password pairing forcing users to use SSO (Single Sign-On) or other methods offered by the service for login;

- Administrators can whitelist domains other than their own so that participants can bypass the waiting room and join the meeting directly;
- Administrators can disable the ability for participants to add notes to a shared screen, acting individually, in groups, or collectively;
- You can now apply the "Unmute All" command to activate the microphone to all participants at once in meetings involving fewer than 200 people;
- Webinar organizers and speakers can eliminate questions and comments sent via Q&A and chat during meetings;
- Users and administrators are now able to set how long Zoom can save data such as call logs, recordings, voice messages, and transcripts.

With significant growth in the last few months, also due to the race to adopt smart working, distance learning, and remote communication solutions, Zoom has found itself in a position to expand its workforce by hiring big shots like Alex Stamos (formerly Facebook), Velchamy Sankarlingam (formerly VMware) and Damien Hooper-Campbell (formerly eBay and Google) to improve the quality and reliability of the service offered.

In the same window as the Waiting Room option is the "Lock Meeting" option. Enabling this will guarantee that no further individuals will be able to barge in, no matter what. This can be useful as, by default, both the host and participants alike have the power to Invite new attendees in (under the Participants tab) at any time. Sure, they'd just get caught by the Waiting Room anyway if enabled, but sometimes one can do without that kind of distraction.

Do not think twice about locking the meeting once all intended attendees are in. As a host, you can unlock the meeting at will, if necessary, ensuring that you're simply keeping trolls out, and not alienating intended participants who just happened to get unlucky with time management.

CHAPTER 2:

App Installation

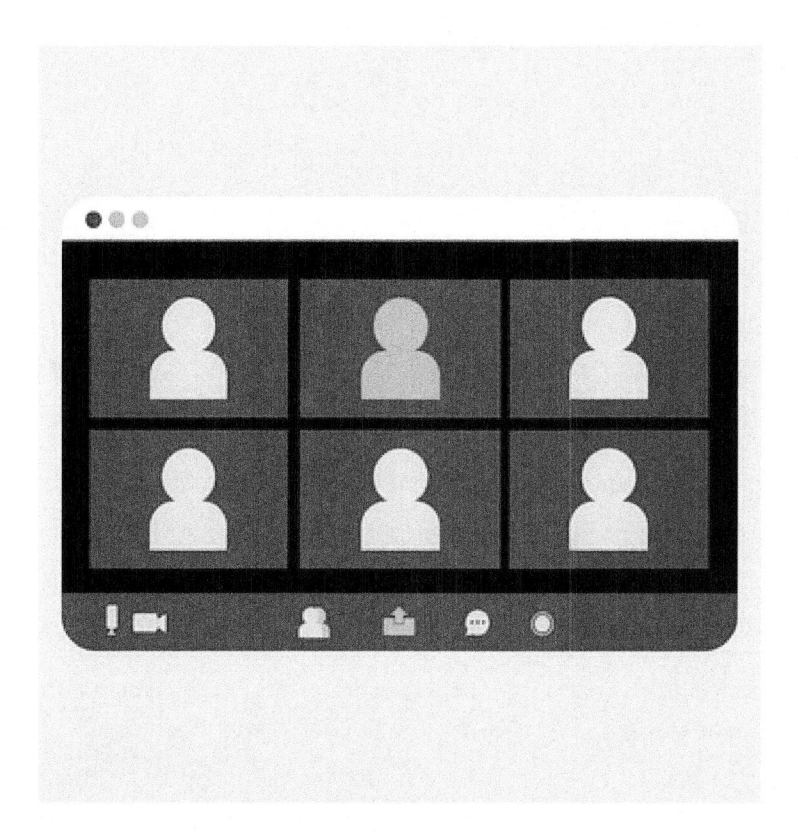

Getting started with zoom

Zoom can also be accessed through its desktop and mobile application version. The desktop app version can be downloaded on Windows and macOS, and the mobile application can be downloaded on iOS and Android.

While it is possible to access any Zoom meeting without signing up and creating an account, it is advisable to sign up using a Google, Facebook, or Zoom account if you will use it frequently. This will make it easier to access every time you want to conduct a meeting.

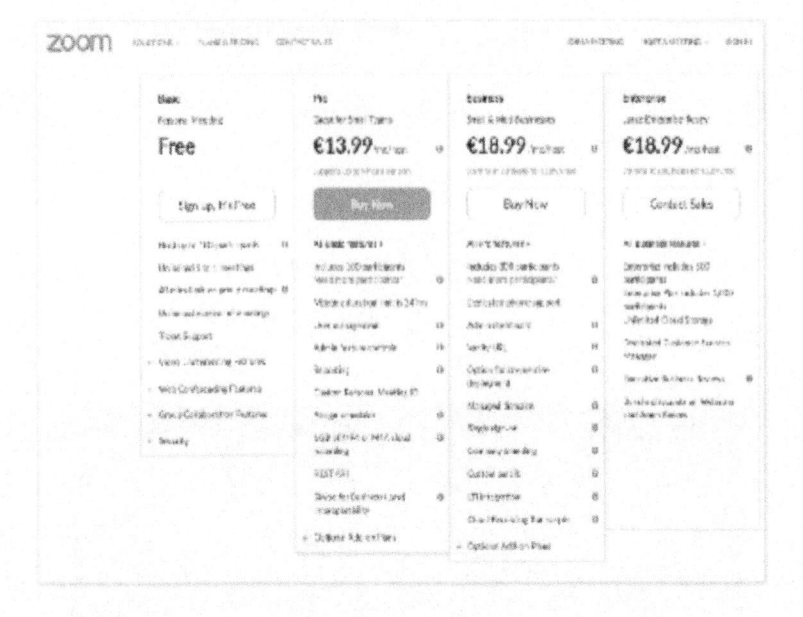

Before we learn about accessing and starting Zoom Meetings, the best way to learn about it is through downloading and installing the Zoom app.

This will simplify its accessibility factor.

Whether you are hosting a meeting or attending as a participant, using Zoom can be extremely effortless once you follow these steps.

Download the App:

To download the Zoom App (desktop or mobile app version), you can *click here* to go to the download page.

Follow the steps and once downloaded on your computer, create an account, or log in with your Facebook or Google account.

Upon using a mobile app, an interface like this will pop up as soon as you enter.

For easier understanding, we are assuming that you are using the desktop version of Zoom.

Start a new meeting

If you are hosting a meeting, click on the 'New Meeting' option that is represented by the orange icon. You will enter an interface that enables you to change the settings according to your preferences.

Audio settings

First, you will tweak the audio settings. To begin with, find the 'Join Audio' at the bottom-left corner of the window and click the arrow beside it. Click on 'Audio Settings' from the dropdown menu.

A 'Settings' window will pop up

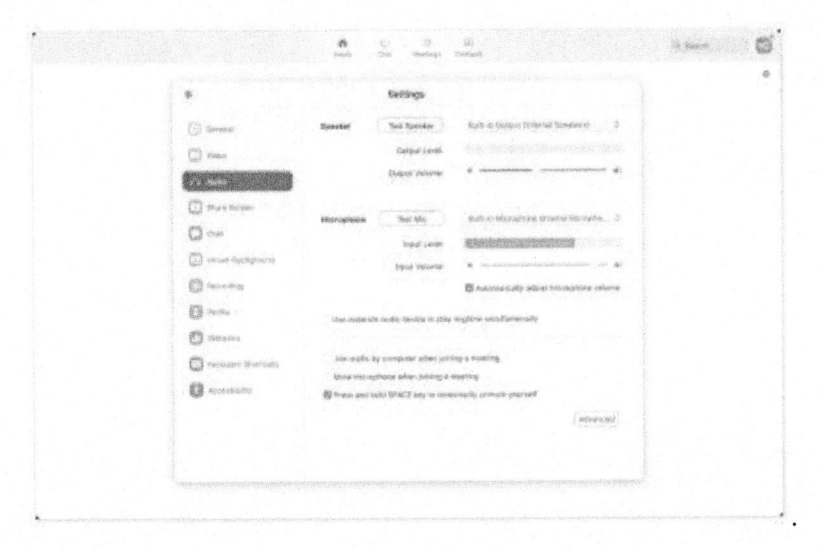

You can always access this window by clicking on the setting icon on the top right part of the screen

Once the window pops up, click on the dropdown list located on the right side of 'Test Speaker' and select the speaker you prefer. You can either choose your headphone jack, your device's speaker, or any other speaker that is linked externally. We would recommend that you wear headphones as it will block out background noise and keep your meeting private if other people are around.

Next, you should check the microphone quality. Click on the dropdown menu on the right side of 'Test Mic.' Depending on the microphone device you are using, select the relevant option. If you have an external microphone connected to your system, the list will display the name. If not, select 'same as the system' to use the device's microphone.

Then, you will check the input level of your microphone and voice quality. Start talking and view the slider besides 'Input Level' as it transitions from red to green. Your audio is stable if you are in the green zone (not too slow and not too loud). Check the box beside 'Automatically adjust microphone volume' to make it easier.

Leave the other settings as they are. You can probably check the box that says 'Join audio by computer when joining a meeting' to access the same setup as soon as you join a call.

Video Settings

Now, we will tweak the video settings. Click on 'Video' located above 'Audio' in the left panel.

The Video Settings box will look like this.

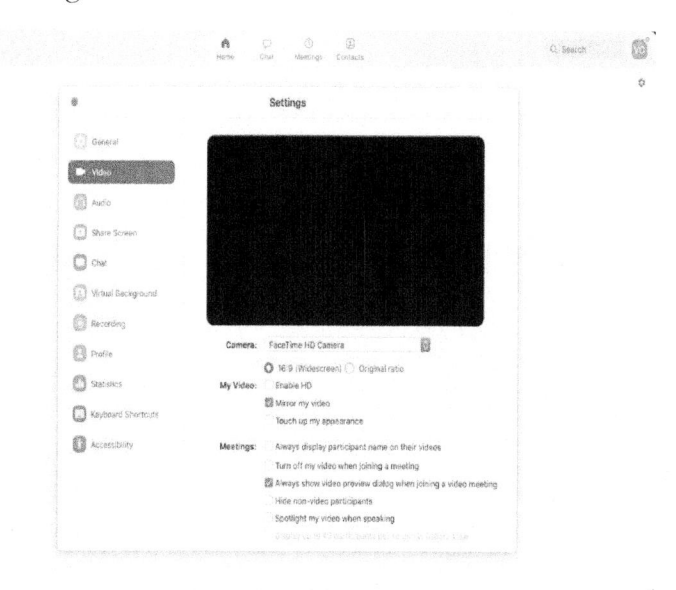

As soon as you click on 'Video', a box appears with a message saying, 'Zoom would like to access the camera.' Click on 'OK.' The black box in this picture will display what is seen by your front-facing camera. This is how the other participants will see you during the call. You can adjust your position and device to provide a clear view.

If you have other devices or webcams attached externally to your video interface, select the device from the dropdown menu beside 'Camera.' Leave the other settings as they are and exit the box.

pag. 226

Stop video option

Once your audio and video settings are in place, you are good to go. Close the setting page and click on the button "New Meeting" to start a meeting. If you need the call to be just audio, you can select the 'Stop Video' option on the bottom-left corner of the window, as you access the meeting.

Invite new participants

The next step will involve inviting participants to the call. Select the 'Participants' option on the bottom panel of the window, and then click on "Invite".

You will see a window that looks like this.

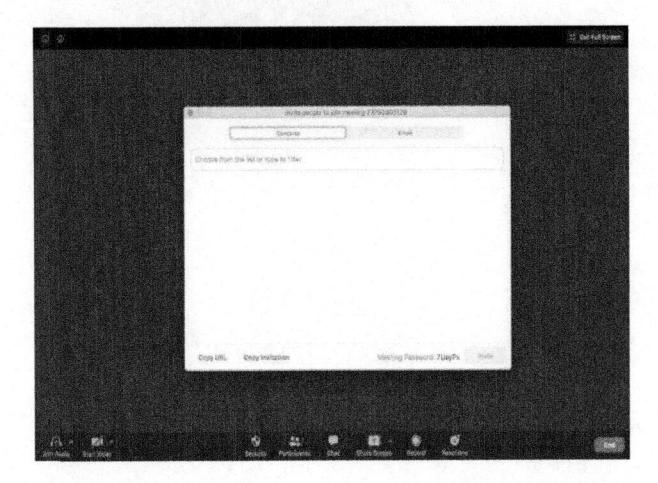

You can either invite people from your contact list or via email. The easiest way is to click on 'Copy URL' and send the generated meeting URL with the people you wish to invite. Exit the box. Once you send this URL to the preferred participants, they can easily access the meeting by pasting this URL in their browser. You can also text or send the meeting password to your participants to join the discussion. We will elaborate further on this later in this section.

Manage participants

We will now manage the participants that have permission to access the meeting. Click on 'Participants' on the bottom panel of the main window.

You will see a popup that will display all the participants that have entered the meeting. It will look like this.

If you move your mouse over the participants' names, you can mute a particular participant or mute all of them by selecting 'Mute All' at the bottom. This functionality is extremely useful when a single person is in need to speak or is instructing everyone.

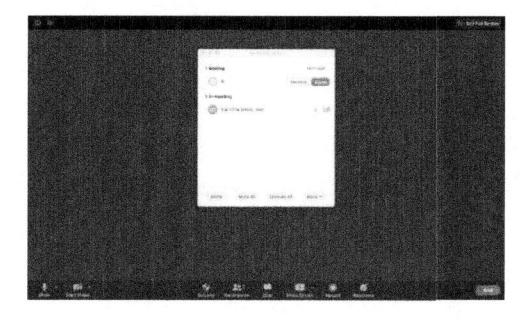

Chat options

Access the 'Chat' option on the bottom of the main window. It will open a popup window. This will allow you to write comments and send messages during the meeting. You can also upload files or photos from your device, Google Drive, or Dropbox by clicking on the file icon.

pag. 228

This is particularly convenient if you want to discuss certain specifications during the meeting, such as presentations, reports, or diagrams. In case you wish to send a private message to a participant you will need to click on "everyone" and select from the list the person that you wish to contact.

Record a meeting

To record the meeting, select 'Record' at the bottom of the main window. As soon as you click the option, you will notice a red pulsing icon in the top-left corner of the window. This signal shows that the meeting is being recorded. The participants will also be aware of the recording as the red icon will be displayed beside your name in the vertical window on the right side of the screen. You can also stop or pause the recording by clicking on the respective buttons beside the recording icon.

To access the recording and choose a particular location to save the recorded data, select 'zoom.us' on the top panel of your window and go to 'Preferences'.

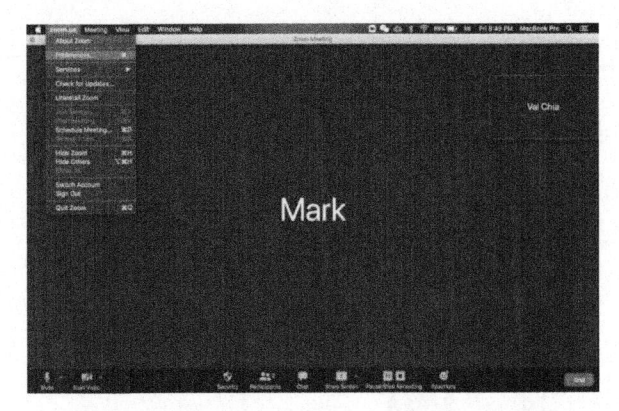

Next, select 'Recording' in the left panel. Click on the list beside 'Store my recordings at,' select 'Choose a new location,' and select the folder or location that will collect all the recordings.

Share your screen

To share your screen with other participants, click on the green icon depicting 'Share Screen' at the bottom of the main window.

A window like this will appear.

When this window pops up, you can choose the desktop or screen that you want to share with others. As soon as you click on 'Share', a window saying 'Allow Zoom to share your screen' will pop up. Click on 'Open System Preferences' and select 'Zoom' from the list.

End the meeting

To end the meeting or the exit, select 'End Meeting,' denoted in red in the bottom-right corner. Select 'End Meeting for All' from the pop-up window to end the meeting.

Schedule a meeting

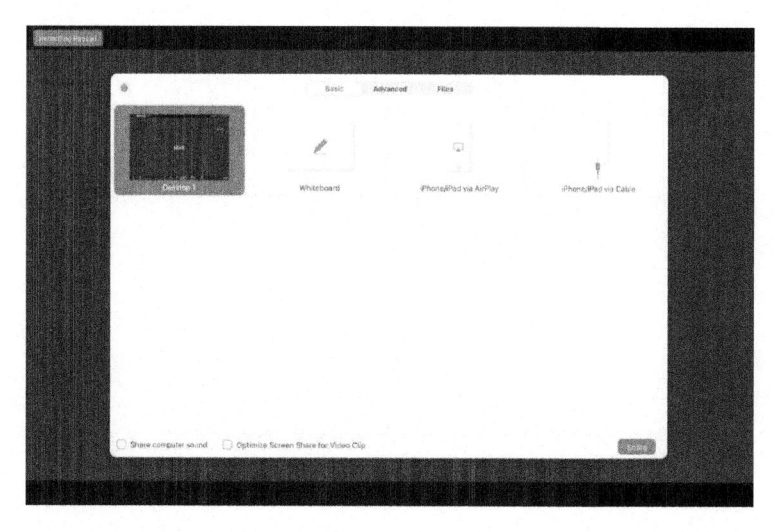

Now let's try scheduling the next meeting, go to the main page of your app, and click on the icon that says 'Schedule.'

You will see a window like this.

Type the name of the subject, class, or topic of discussion of the meeting in the 'Topic' box. Select the starting and ending date and time of the meeting. Since we are learning the features on the free version of Zoom, you can set only 40 minutes. To increase the duration, go to the official website and buy a subscription plan that offers longer meetings and additional benefits.

Next, select the box beside 'Generate Automatically' under 'Meeting ID' (this should be your preferred option).

Then, generate a password by checking the box beside 'Require meeting password.' Type a password of your choosing and share it with the other participants to give them access to the meeting. By unchecking the box, anyone can access the meeting without a password, so it's always preferable to create a password.

Next, you can select whether you want your video to be on or off during the meeting. You also have the option to choose whether you want your participants' video to be on or off.

For the audio, select 'Telephone and Computer Audio,' as some of your participants might use their phone and cellular data if they don't have a stable broadband connection.

You can add this schedule reminder on a calendar of your choice. Choose among iCal, Google Calendar, or any other calendar that you use.

Lastly, click on Advanced Options and select your preferred option among 'Enable waiting room' (lets your participants wait before starting the meeting), 'Enable join before host' (lets your participants enter the meeting before you do), 'Mute participants on entry' (mutes all participants until you enter and unmute), and 'Record the meeting automatically on the local computer' (begins recording without selecting the option).

Once you select the appropriate options, click on 'Schedule' and your meeting will be noted on your calendar. When you open your calendar, you will receive the details regarding the meeting, including the meeting ID, password, and even a mobile tap feature that takes you to the meeting directly if accessed through a cell phone. Send this auto-generated message containing the meeting details to your desired participants through e-mail or text.

Homepage Options

A few more options that can be accessed from the home page (located on the top of the page) include:

- **Chat:** If you have made a few friends on Zoom and added them, they will appear on this Chat on a panel. You can directly chat with them through this option.
- **Meetings:** With this option, you can check all the meetings that you have scheduled for a future date or the ones that have been scheduled for you by someone else. The panel will also show your Personal Meeting ID or PMI. With your PMI, you can use options such as Copy Invitation, Edit, or Join from a Room.
- **Contacts:** You can view your added contacts in this panel, both from your directory and channels.

- **Your profile:** You can change your profile settings by selecting your picture icon on the top-right corner of the home page. This is your avatar. You can add a personal note, set your status as Away, Available, or Do Not Disturb (you can choose the duration), make changes to your profile, and upgrade to the Pro version.

Zoom main features

Zoom has many features that make the app desirable and well enough to compete with other video conferencing tools. These features range from the user's ability to share files; share screens while working and record audio and video during meetings. With the increasing demands for Zoom, developers have up their games to ensure users' satisfaction comes first while maintaining the product's long-standing integrity. The following features are common in zoom meetings:

Zoom Room controller

To have access to the Zoom control board, your device must be on either of the following OS; apple iPad running on iOS version 8.0 and above; android tablet running OS 4.0 and above, windows tablet running version 10.0.14393 or later, Crestron Mercury.

You need to download the zoom Room controller from the Zoom download page. The following features are accessible with the Zoom Room controller;

- Meet now
- Schedule meeting now with a selected number of participants.
- Contact list display for participants.
- Meeting list
- Display today's meetings list of participants
- Get upcoming meeting alerts.
- Joining a meeting

- Join a meeting using the meeting ID.

Presentation

- Start your meeting while still sharing the screen.
- Set screen sharing duration

Phone

- Switching from a phone Zoom call to a video session.
- Show call history.
- Device settings
- Select microphone
- Select speakers
- Web settings
- Private meeting
- Hide meeting ID.

Zoom visitor control

The first thing you must ensure is that you have total control of your screen during meetings. You must deploy strategies to keep sanity in the meeting room. This is where visitor control comes in. You do not want a case of Zoom bombing where unwanted visitors are gate crashing your meeting and sharing unsavory contents.

You can control the visitor's presence before the meeting and even after the meeting using your *host control bar*. To prevent unnecessary sharing of contents by visitors, make use of the host control bar.

Tap the arrow beside the share screen menu to take you to the advanced sharing option. Locate the "who can share screen and choose" the only host."

As part of Zoom's effective management of visitors and participants. There are features you must take note of. Follow these steps below to manage visitors effectively:

- Authorize the meeting so that only the invited participants can log in with their email.
- Generate a random Zoom meeting ID for all meetings. This will prevent gatecrashes.
- Remove recalcitrant participants
- Disable video access to your meeting.
- Disallow private chat.
- Use the waiting room.

Zoom Virtual Background

Instead of using the default Zoom background during Zoom meetings, you can make use of virtual backgrounds that can be downloaded online - or from your device pictures or videos. This works better with a green screen and a well-lighted room.

How to enable virtual background in zoom;

- Navigate to the Zoom web as an administrator and click on the Account settings icon.
- Enable the virtual background settings by navigating to the virtual background option.
- Activated.
- How to enable virtual background for group members
- Login to the Zoom web portal as an admin to edit users' group.
- Select the group management icon.
- Tap the name of the group and pick the settings icon.
- Enable the virtual background settings on the meeting tab.
- How to enable virtual background for personal use
- Enter the Zoom Web Portal.

- Access the "my meeting settings icon" if you are the administrator of "meeting settings icon" if you're an ordinary member.
- Enable the virtual background settings on the meeting tab.

To enable a virtual background for the Zoom room.

- Login to the Zoom Web Portal as an administrator.
- Enter the zoom room page and check-in account settings.
- Turn on the virtual background with a green screen.
- You can add more background pictures from your device's library if you want.
- To enable a virtual background on windows.
- Log in to the Zoom desktop client.
- Tap on your profile picture and choose settings.
- Select virtual background
- Toggle on" I have a green screen" if you already have it set up.
- Select your desired virtual background image from the available ones. You can as well add them from your device's gallery.

Break out rooms

The Zoom breakout rooms allow hosts to split zoom sessions into more than one session. It is only the account owner that can have access to this feature.

To enable Zoom breakout rooms for all the members in your group:

- Login into the Zoom web as an administrator that has the privilege to edit groups.
- Access the navigation menu and click User Management and then Group Management.
- Tap the name of the group, then choose the Settings tab.

- Scroll down to the Breakout Room option on the Meeting tab to enable it
- To enable zoom break out room for your personal use.
- Login to the Zoom portal.
- Click Account Management from the navigation menu, and then click on Account Settings (provided that you're the administrator of the account) or Settings (if you are an account member).
- Enable the Breakout Room option on the Meeting tab.

Zoom Share Screen

The Zoom share screen is a common feature on zoom for PC, tablets, and mobile devices. This feature allows participants to share what's on their screen for easy access by the group members. Co-workers, while working from home, can receive instructions and teach one another using their Zoom share screen. With this feature, you can see what the other members are doing on their computer screen. Only that the shared screen can only be done by the host if the account is basic. For premiums accounts, the host and the attendees can both share their screens. The hosts do not necessarily need to grant access before other members can share their screens.

How to share screen on Windows and Mac.
- Locate the share screen icon in the meeting control
- Choose the screen you want to share. You can even share the Microsoft documents screen when opened.
- Tap the share icon to start sharing.
- The share screen will take up all your screen. You can exit the full-screen mode by clicking on the exit full-screen icon.
- While sharing your screen, you can access the following menus;
- Mute or unmute your microphone.
- Start or stop your video.

- If you are the host, you can view or manage the participants.
- Begin a new screen sharing.
- Pause your screen sharing mode
- Invite other participants to join your current meeting.
- Record the meeting to your computer storage or the Zoom Cloud.
- End the meeting at any time you want.
- Turn on the dual monitor option to be able to see both the participants and the screen you're sharing at the same time.

How to share your screen on Android devices:
Sharing screen on Android requires Android 5.0 and later:

- In the meeting Control, click on the share icon.
- A prompt will come up asking you which content you want to share. Choose the content you want to share.
- You can share photos, documents, whiteboards, website addresses, etc.

Sharing screens.

- Click the share icon in the meeting control.
- A list of available sharing options will be displayed. Choose screen.
- Click on "start now" to start.
- You can choose to share anything from your phone's desktop while zoom keeps running in the background.
- You can stop sharing by tapping on stop share at the bottom of your screen.

How to share your screen on iOS:
Needs iOS 11 or higher. You can share photos, iCloud Drive, Dropbox, whiteboard, etc. You can disallow any of these features from your account settings under the integration menu.

pag. 238

To share content

- Click on share content directly from the meeting control.
- Select the category of content you want to share.
- If it is a document, you want to share, select the document, and choose the document from your Google drive.

To share the screen:

- Select the sharing icon and choose the share screen.

Zoom Whiteboard

The Zoom whiteboard feature will give access to you (the host) and group members to share a virtual whiteboard with annotations. It works best on Zoom for Windows, Zoom for Mac, Linux, iPad, and Android.

Sharing a whiteboard on Windows:

- Tap the share screen icon in the toolbar.
- Select whiteboard
- Choose shares.
- The annotations tools will be displayed. You can show and hide them from the whiteboard option
- Create and switch between pages by using the page control icon located at the bottom right corner of your whiteboard.
- Stop sharing when you are done.

Sharing whiteboard on Android:

- Navigate to the meeting control and click on share.
- Choose the share whiteboard menu.

- Tap the icon that looks like a pen at the extreme left of the screen. This will open the annotation tools for writing and editing.
- Click on the pen icon again when you are done to close annotation.
- Stop sharing.

Sharing whiteboard on iOS: whiteboard only works on iPad for now, and not on iPhone.

- Click on share content available in the meeting control menu.
- Select the whiteboard.
- The annotation tools will come up where you can edit and write texts.
- Tap "stop share" to stop sharing the whiteboard.

Zoom record meeting

Tapping the record button at the bottom of your screen can enable you to record a meeting in Zoom.

Recording meeting in zoom is good, particularly if there is a particular colleague that should be in the meeting but was unable absent for one reason or another.

The individual can always listen to the recording later to understand what has been discussed during the meeting.

The organizer of the meeting must give access before you can record the meeting on zoom. If the organizer does not grant access, I am afraid it will be difficult to record such a meeting.

Zoom recording on PC
Tap the recording button at the bottom of your screen to start recording. Tap stop to end recording. The file will be stored as an MP4 on your computer.

Zoom recording on Android and iOS

The same procedure is followed to record in both Android and iPhone devices. You must be on the Pro plan before you have access to the record. Besides, the meeting planner must grant you access.

Open your Zoom app on Android or iPhone to join an ongoing meeting. Click on the three dots at the extreme right corner of your screen. Select record to the cloud (if you are using iPhone) or record (for Android).

You can stop recording when you are done.

Zoom chat

The Zoom chat is a new addition from Zoom to allow business users to chat securely. The chats are stored in local drives or Zoom clouds. Zoom chats add to the complete zoom package where users can access real-time messaging platforms and share business ideas. The Zoom chat is available on both the mobile version and the desktop version. There is a premium account and a free account. Channels on premium accounts can have up to 5000 members or more while the free chat is limited to 500 persons. The Zoom chats are end-to-end encrypted; you do not need to worry about the security of data.

Zoom Remote control

The Zoom remote control allows participants to control each other's screens while granting access. You can request remote control from the organizer who is sharing his screen. When he grants access, users can have the liberty to control what is happening on their screen.

How to request remote control on windows and Mac:

- Tap the view option drop-down menu to select request remote control.

- After the host grant access, you can then start controlling his screen by tapping inside the screen share.
- To stop remote control, tap the view option drop-down again and choose to give up the remote control.

RICHARD V. ROSS

CHAPTER 3:

Zoom For Teachers

Symmetric class meetings, through which everybody logs in at a pre-scheduled time to a cloud conferencing program, are one way to create interest and promote collaboration in your complete online courses. Teachers can use a web-conference program in a synchronous session and allow all the students to participate at a pre-scheduled date. The application for video conferencing at the university is Zoom. Zoom may be found on computers, desktops, iPad, smartphones, and even cell devices, enabling students to navigate the class session in several respects.

As a teacher, whether you or your learners have a condition that prevents you from meeting face to face, Zoom will help to keep your class running. Concurrent online class meetings, where everybody is expected to attend a Zoom group, are one way to build interaction while students are far away. Still, Zoom may also be used to help special education and learning situations. Zoom may be used on any device and even workstation phones, allowing students to connect with the team meeting in many ways. You can find tips on planning for your Zoom meetings in this chapter, including gathering students with the conversation, screen editing, polling, non-verbal reviews and breakdown rooms, and supplying your community with open online learning sessions, as well as resources for different teaching scenarios.

Preparing for Class

Zoom was developed with creativity. Now, if you make confident important choices and familiarize yourself with the application before welcoming students into an informal conference, it works better. Zoom's free edition can provide you with the best performance and features while holding a Class.

Coach the students to have Zoom activated.

Students preparing to attend Zoom meetings from a Laptop or computer will also access the application from the Zoom website.

- Get to learn the controls on the server.
- Catch up on managing a quick Zoom meeting.
- Sign up to work out.
- Check the recording and the audio.
- Visit zoom.us/test to confirm the internet, video, and audio connections.
- When there are several meeting participants in the same area, only one person can enter the conference with audio to prevent suggestions.
- Find the source of light.
- Make sure a source of light should be in front of you and not behind you.

pag. 245

Schedule Class

Zoom provides a platform for webinars and conferences. All formats help you to communicate with students, although some variations do occur. To pick the style that fits better for you, choose the Zoom flowchart or webinar/meeting comparison chart. Go to the Navigation section to the Zoom feature, press Plan a New Conference and obey the directions.

- Enable your device with the Zoom Windows software.
- Tap at the upper left on "Back".
- Tap "Schedule".
- Enter all related information such as day, year, subject, etc.
- Select your favorite digital calendar (Google Calendar is perfect if you have got Mail or email accounts), and you will be brought to a page with your Zoom connection.
- You may give the connection to your students in the meeting scheduler of your online calendar.
- When applicable, choose regular meetings such that the URL can stay the same over the course. Try to place a positive name on your conferences. Meetings of the course occur inside the platform of the Zoom course.

Recordings can be made accessible automatically via the course page.

The course meetings can be separated from other conferences.

Planned meetings often serve as activities for Calendar class participants.

For unplanned events, simply use your meeting ID and official Zoom URL. Such gatherings are not going to have the advantages mentioned earlier, so cannot be hosted by someone else.

Plan Roles

Assigning specific tasks to the students may be an efficient means of coordinating group practice. Often certain students take too much accountability for the activity of a community, while others may be hesitant to commit to the activities of the group. Assigning responsibilities helps to spread liability among group members and guarantees transparency for the involvement of all students. As students practice various roles, they have the chance to develop a wide range of competencies.

The most needed positions for group work include facilitator, planner, and organizer, timekeeper, and issue manager. You would want to create notes of what it feels like when the job is done well when it is not done well. Ask the students to comment on their perspectives operating in communities in writing or solving issues. Students might still have suggestions for different assigned positions. When you appoint someone else to handle facets of digital rooms, you will have a less challenging classroom managerial experience. Try requesting one supervisor or student to track the conversation and one to assist their peers with difficulties with technology. Formal identification of alternate hosts may also be created. This way, you will focus on giving lectures and offer some additional technical skills to the students.

Enhance Student's Sense of Community

If everybody reveals their faces through their webcam, the feeling of presence is strengthened. Suggest asking students to click on film as a core component of attendance, because if you can see them, it becomes simpler to communicate with the class, so students are more willing to pay care because they realize they are on display.

Train students even about how to turn to the view of the Gallery (this is the perspective where everybody is equally accessible to one another).

Suggestions to connect with your students:

- Make eye contact with the camera.
- Mute mics in case you do not participate.
- Find the illumination! Make sure a bright light is in front of you and not behind you.
- Talk in a conversational way-you does not need to talk up.
- Read on to operate a seamless meeting in Zoom for further information.

A good sense of community can boost the class online and lead to student achievement. The culture can be improved if you take action to keep it protected from harassment or disturbance. A few approaches to meet such targets are here:

Introduce yourself with the safe Zoom Meetings setups and guidance.

Using the regional meeting configuration and in-meeting guidelines to ensure the class is attended only by enrolled learners and invited visitors.

Manage Technical Problems

For every video conferencing program, the three most important technological problems are:

- Members could not see.
- Members could not hear.
- External noise and mic problems.

You can overcome technical issues by hosting an online training meeting for reduced stakes, with the primary aim of signing in, troubleshooting technological issues, and getting accustomed to the Zoom application. Get in your meeting early enough to sort out technical problems. Provide a contingency strategy in case of unknown complications or challenges. Students are informed of the backup plan in advance so that if technical issues arise, they can stay on task.

Know how to address these problems by troubleshooting issues. Try communicating with your community the Participant's Guide for enhancing Your Zoom Performance. It is recommended to host an online discussion experience with low-stakes introductory meetings, whose primary purpose is to have an entire team login, diagnose problems, technical issues, and get used to Zoom functionality.

Create a Teaching Agenda

Prepare for a simultaneous training session online much as you would prepare for an in-person meeting. Discuss the plan with students in advance, and students do have a good understanding of how the curriculum is going to proceed, what is going to be discussed and the events they are going to compete in. Periodically review web behavior and student aspirations or recommend providing the "**good management**" guide detailing goals.

Plan for a concurrent session of the course much as you would prepare for knowledge gives the lesson.

Here is a testing agenda for a simultaneous sixty-minute instructor meeting to share your agenda with students in advance, so they know what is coming:

- Make students reflect on a problem before joining the digital classroom and write their answers on the whiteboard.
- Using the polling method to ask a question that includes and decides personal significance for the Mini-reading subject.
- Link computer launches PowerPoint and offers mini-readings. To mark the PowerPoint slides, use the Annotation functionality in Zoom.
- Render the survey issue provisionally.

- Assign students to separate breakout spaces, chat for ten minutes, and develop a shared Google Report.
- Ask each party to appoint a delegate, to sum up, the main points of their debate.
- Ask students to support conversation if they are always puzzled.
- Clear up misunderstandings found in the muddiest point conversation.
- Summarize the session's tasks, set goals for the follow-up events, and achieve them.

Record your Class

If somebody has a technological problem, you can offer them further access to the course work. You should report the class session to counter this.

Record on the web, not on your desktop: Recording in the cloud is easy because you will access both a video URL and an online transcribed clip. Zoom recordings do not have a quota, so records of meetings sessions using Zoom can surface only a few hours.

Begin recording in the appropriate style: Once you start recording, the recording interface is focused on your vision. Note to swap presentations and turn to an active speaking view rather than a gallery (or do not use the camera or anything), or you will be overlaid in the clip over the upper right corner.

While recording your class, keep in mind certain things;

- Let the students know that you will be recording the class.
- Give students a choice to silence their audio when filming and switching off their camera.
- When meetings are captured in the cloud, and you use a module, the recordings can be located right in the PC.

- Such records could be done to specific preservation procedures than other documentation of class sessions.
- For advice about where to place the recordings, and how to show them to your students, contact your local university development help.

Specific Teaching Scenario

If you are the one who is assigned to take notes (a great practice in usability), you should create closed captions, enabling you to translate what is being said in real-time. Zoom conveniently combines with services such as Play Media when you require live annotations. Prices for such a provision are not directly provided. Many students cannot see the graphic presentation or make sense of it as you wish. Take the habit of conceptually describing what happens on the screen.

Small-Group Discussions

Screen sharing may be used to collaborate with a person or group of students to discuss the course. Approving remote screen monitoring enables one to take possession of the interactive program of the other, which allows the remote device to browse, enter code, etc. Remember that your Breakout Room configuration will be deactivated when remote screen control is available. Collaborative problem sharing and brainstorming are effective to annotate a whiteboard, using the virtual whiteboard application digitally. Allow everyone to annotate on the same platform in the session to express ideas and methods for solving problems. A screen is handwriting support.

You can use the high-quality audio and footage from Zoom to easily have a conversation with a person or student community. Share documents or something else on your device conveniently via sharing a screen to support your discussion in an online class. The waiting room presents you with a single Zoom user ID and the option to invite-only chosen individuals to the conversation. In your waiting area, you can even set up a personalized greeting that lets students realize you will be seeing them early. Start small discussions when most students join your meeting.

Zoom Assignment Setup

Instructors have the option to set up a Task or Debate Board in all courses and encourage students to download or submit a file. Large recording files may take up a lot of room in the course, or the submitting region of the student's program. There is a specific feature for Zoom videos that will guarantee students can reduce their number of files to a minimum.

The application is recognized as the Media Record/Upload method. It would require students to upload five hundred Megabytes files without restricting either the course or the students.

Setting up an Assignment or Discussion forum post with these resources, and having the students know the correct way to apply is particularly crucial for the teacher. Do not search the "Data Uploads" box when setting up the assignment because the students would use up much of the course room. Alternatively, you can allow the "Record/Upload Files" feature to avoid massive uploads of files for your task. If you duplicate Assignments from previous classes, you will still need to change them.

Upload Assignment on Zoom

When you have chosen the "File on this Device" choice to document your presentation, using the steps below to transfer your file to an Assignment. Your professor will provide the task that is designed to take a Zoom recording.

You should not add a Zoom link to a request that has a click "Link Upload".

- Select "Send Application" to start Notification.
- Select "Media track/Upload".
- Choose the tab "Upload files" then press the button "Download video file".
- Using the Zoom Data File on your Windows.
- Select on "Deliver Assignment".

Engaging Students Using Different Features

No one likes sitting through a normal classroom lecture for sixty minutes, and the reality that you have all the teachers there and present does not influence such a class session structure. You may use the Zoom functions to direct various kinds of interactive tasks. Such tasks provide flexibility to break up a long-class session and provide diverse forms of communicating themselves.

Chat

Using the chat platform will promote interaction by encouraging students to connect, rather than only listen, with the live operation. Also, Chat has advantages over conventional classrooms: Get vast quantities of replies to a question right away, then use those answers in need or save them for later. See just where the students feel on a specific topic of discussion, advising them who to contact next.

Think about when, or where to allow students to talk. Are you happy with feedback during the class in chat, for example, or just at specific points? If you have a supervisor that can delete comments, you can require students to chat on an ongoing basis; otherwise, you can promote its usage at distinct times. Chat enables posts to be submitted to the whole community or another user. If you want to hold the record, you may access the complete chat history of the lesson.

For students, chatting can be unbearable. It is advised that you provide this form of interaction as an alternative, but not all students need it. Even chat can be challenging to track when you are still attempting to lecture. Provide a student or supervisor supervising the conversation so that you can concentrate on teaching. Recreate live posting on twitter of guest lectures as a way to gather questions and answer them at the end of the meeting. Select one student to track the conversation when they come in and to compile queries.

Create a simulated team, where a selected community of students collaborates to solve a question or address an issue.

The other students respond via the chat communications channel to contributions with their fellow students.

Invite students to record questions as small groups during your classes and invite one student to address them for community discussion.

Screen Sharing and Annotation

Zoom provides simple annotation resources that can be used to direct or illustrate an idea to students. Use such resources by choosing the choice Annotate while viewing the display. Computer annotations were not open to those of screen readers. When you are utilizing this tool, make sure to follow best practices for open presentation: explain what you are doing when you are doing it (for example, "drawing a huge red ring around the registration form on this new website").

Sharing the screens is very important to show to your students to enhance your teaching skills and your students' learning ability. You will share the computer screen with anyone at the Zoom meeting using this icon of screen sharing. Sharing a screen with Zoom is simple; all you have to do is press on the "Share Screen" link at the bottom of your conference. You will then press on the device you would like to display. Its modern technology and infinite functionality which help students in their classroom are becoming more efficient and imaginative.

Polling

Engagement in a virtual class is a core aspect of student performance. Try integrating polling functionality into difficult concepts to improve student interest with your online course. Polling enables students to share their experiences and communicate with each other, and often tells coordinators about the students in the class and encourages them to set the stage for a positive segment further. For an online course, surveys are an essential method, as they can:

- Link students in the classroom so that they can express their views on different topics.
- Be more interactive in introducing a topic or action.
- Give useful information on the readiness and progress of the students.
- Help guide and concentrate students on their education.

Polls are simple to set up and then use and will bring value to an online course. A teacher is provided with several ways to incorporate this practice into Zoom. Set up polling ahead of time and start them in your class meeting.

Non-Verbal Feedback

Significant feedback on assignments promotes analytical thought, proactive practice, and establishes relationships between teacher and student, which are vital in an online setting. Although feedback helps evaluation, improvement, and enhancement of results, it often improves student enthusiasm when they believe that the teacher is involved in their progress.

To encourage students to connect with the coaching staff without disturbing the class, enable the non-verbal input function for your meetings. Check-in with the students regularly to answer any non-verbal suggestions.

This app also helps you to handle vocal input, since students will be told to use the "lift hand" function to signal when they want to talk. Need to make students quiet before you order them to remove outside input from the room.

Breakout Rooms

Breakout Rooms encourage you to divide the meeting into several meetings, in a live classroom environment, comparable to community breakout sessions. Students should create their social groups and would promote further interaction. You will use the versatility of the breakout rooms in Zoom to help students perform collective learning. As the teacher, when it is time to rebuild, you can enter the breakout rooms, relay notices to the breakdown rooms, and finish the breakdown session.

Zoom Individual Presentation Setup

Allow the time to customize the external atmosphere before you present a specific presentation. If necessary, prepare a document of the conversation with a microphone because such microphones will eliminate noise not coming from three to five meters away from the mouthpiece. Use a space where you can shut the door or not be disrupted while minimizing audio from elsewhere in the room. Tiled rooms are recommended over wooden floors to lessen the noise effect in your audiotape. When you capture the video image, sunlight will be coming from in front of you and never behind you to stop putting shadows on your eyes.

One or two crane lamps are lined up behind the screen monitor, and you will be doing this conveniently facing it. Your backdrop should be fascinating but not intrusive, and it does not include a window if the window has both shutters and curtains to obstruct the light. While capturing, mute the mobile phones, email updates, text messages/chats, and other electronic signals. Many vibratory alerts from cell phones are visible when using the smartphone microphone, so you may need to put your mobile phone on a comforter or smooth surface to minimize this

Professional and personal distance

In an ideal case, all communication between the student and teacher would take place using school property, such as an LMS. In reality, not all school districts have an LMS that can accommodate video and audio communication. Furthermore, not all LMS have appropriate "push" notification or message sending capabilities. If the message is purely confined to the LMS and the student never logs into the LMS system, he or she will never see the message.

On the other hand, if you interjected your feedback on last night's homework question into a student's social media feed, you might have a better chance of reaching the student in a timely fashion. However, this breaches the distinction between personal and professional communication. Text messages and messaging services such as WhatsApp can also breach this divide.

Some students and teachers can easily separate a school-based discussion in one chat window from a casual conversation in a neighboring chat window. Others cannot. Reduce the risk of unwanted and inappropriate communication by making it clear that the communication you use is for professional purposes.

Email is the middle ground because email is frequently used for both personal and professional communication. Using school resources, such as the LMS or school email address would be preferred.

However, if you must use common platforms such as Gmail or Discord, you can still try to delineate the professional nature of the communication channel. Don't use your personal Gmail address. Obtain a new one that relates to school. Johnnydoe@gmail.com sounds like a personal address. MrDoe-MercyHigh@gmail.com marks itself as a school-centric email address. You can similarly name Discord channels or other meeting places to remind everyone about the nature of the communication.

The content of your messages can also breach the personal-professional divide. Some teachers like to build rapport with students with casual conversations, jokes, and a more approachable personality. That's great, and I'm not saying that you can't do that, but you need to remind the students that they are communicating with you for education. When you are physically within a classroom surrounded by other students, the context is obvious. Teachers stand at the head of the class. Students sit in desks. All communication takes place within this context. When a student is texting you while reclining on a sofa in his living room, context can be lost easily.

Students engage in inappropriate behavior, such as asking a teacher on a date, but the context of a classroom surrounded by other students meant that the behavior could be defused easily. Everyone, including the instigating student, understood the absurdity of his behavior. A joke, however inappropriate on the student's behalf, was more likely to remain a joke because the context of the situation was inescapable.

Don't let your students or you lose the context. You can achieve this by making sure the context of your online communication is always distinct from personal and casual communication. Even something as small as using proper grammar and punctuation in your messages can help with this. On the other hand, some educators advise that you should use smiley faces and emoticons to connect better with your students. Every situation is different, and what's appropriate in one situation might not be in another. What works in a college course doesn't necessarily work in elementary school.

But in all situations, I encourage you to put as much distance between your professional and personal communication channels as you reasonably can, however, you view and define those terms. These demarcations should also be apparent to the students, and by doing so, you set up clearly defined norms, which is the subject of the next section.

A final suggestion is that group meetings are usually more professional than one-on-one meetings. There are accountability and a common agenda. Instead of meeting with students individually online, consider setting up small groups of appointments or office hours for more personalized, yet professional, discussions, and feedback.

Define a primary communication channel

Consider what happens if a student has a question about a homework assignment during the evening. In a traditional classroom setting, student-teacher interaction takes place during the school day. Most, but not all, students would not even think to call or email their teacher late at night over a difficult homework question.

However, what happens in a distance learning environment? In an asynchronous setting, students access pre-recorded videos and download assignments at their schedule. There's no context of "school hours" outside what their parents might enforce. In that case, a student might be more inclined to send an email at midnight, when he's working on his assignment. What's the expectation for you, the teacher? Are you supposed to reply to this email as soon as you see it? Within one hour? By the next working day—when the student may have moved on to something else, reducing the quality of the engagement?

It's impossible to be available for twenty-four hours. You're a teacher, not an emergency room doctor. Define clear communication channels between yourself and your students, and make sure your students follow those channels. If students disregard your guidelines, remind them, and nudge them back into the norms. Stand by the lines you draw; you're not helping your students by encouraging undisciplined violation of rules. If your course materials are primarily asynchronous, it would make sense to set up office hours, daily or weekly as it makes sense for you and your students. Do keep in mind that older students have multiple classes and multiple teachers, all with competing workloads. An in-person high school schedule automatically makes sure there are no time conflicts between courses. In the case of a sudden switch to distance learning, the history teacher may have reserved Wednesday mornings, the math teachers want to hold office hours at one in the afternoon each day, and the music teacher is experimenting with a virtual orchestra on Friday mornings.

Consult your students. Offer more than the minimum office hours so that they have a choice of which session to attend in case of conflicts.

Another approach is to have students register in advance for time slots. This prevents you from wasting time sitting around if no one is going to show up. I would discourage one-on-one video chats, but you can instead have group signups, or consolidate the time slots so that three to four people show up for them.

Even if you offer synchronous class time, students may still have questions outside the allotted hours. In that case, designate a primary channel of communication. Email is the obvious choice, with an LMS-integrated messaging, or at least a professional email, being preferable as described earlier in this book. Set clear expectations. Will you reply to emails between nine in the morning and five in the evening? Tell the students upfront what they can expect. If the email arrives after five in the evening, let them know that you are unlikely to respond to it until the next morning.

And if you have homework deadlines, be sure to include the specific time on the due date. Such expectations apply to students, too. If you email a student, what happens if he doesn't reply, or replies after three days?

You can make it clear from the outset that you expect all emails to be professionally handled, which means replies within one day at most. You could even use emails to evaluate a participation grade, with deadlines for replies. Compared to normal email use, that might sound strict, but let's be realistic. If you sent an email to thirty responsible, working adults asking for feedback within one day, how many would reply on time? Now consider the same scenario for young students at home with little accountability.

That brings us to the next section about accountability.

Define clear norms

Norms, or standards of behavior, in a classroom are clear to most students and teachers because of years of repeated practice:

- Students sit at desks. Teachers sit or stand at the front.
- If a student wants to speak or has a question, he raises his hand. While the teacher is speaking, students are expected to be quiet. This can, of course, change if the teacher opens the class up to discussion or if the teaching style facilitates casual and frequent dialogue.
- If a student wants to use the restroom, he signs out or takes a hall pass specifically for that purpose. Only one student can leave the class in this fashion at a time.
- Shouting, using a phone, throwing things—these are generally prohibited.
- Some teachers may allow drinking or food during class. In elementary schools, a specific snack or break time may be set aside.
- Students refer to teachers by their last names.
- Students don't curse, use obscenities, or slang when speaking in class.
- Students dress appropriately, defined by the school dress code or the need to be non-distracting to other students.

The above list is hardly exhaustive or uniform among classrooms, but it represents some common standards of behavior.

When switching to an online environment, there can be confusion about the norms. This confusion is exacerbated if casual and professional communication channels are intermingled.

As an example, imagine that the teacher creates a public social media profile to distribute course materials. A common use case is to upload videos to YouTube. What are the norms for student behavior in this case? Will the teacher moderate the comments below the video? If a student makes an inappropriate remark, will the teacher seek disciplinary action? What if a student shares a link in the comments to a site that you haven't vetted? What if a student asks a question—should you, the teacher, be expected to reply to the YouTube comment immediately? What if you never see the comment?

Another example is using a group webcam sharing technology such as Zoom. Who is allowed to type into the common chat area, and when? Who is allowed to make voice comments, and when? Do students always need to show their faces on the camera? What if a student needs to leave during the middle of class? What if a student is not paying attention?

Proper classroom behavior in an online setting can be unclear to both your students and you. If there's a mismatch of expectations, that can ruin the quality of engagement.

Here are some suggestions for setting up norms for distance learning engagement.

Greater distance requires greater accountability

Fostering engagement with your students is critical to success in distance learning, but there's one big caveat: Your students have to show up for you to engage with them.

There's a world of difference for accountability in distance learning versus in-person classes, which tends to have a very negative effect on education if you don't take special care to address this issue. While the most disciplined and motivated students may perform the same, or even better, in an online teaching environment, most students will face some, if not substantial, difficulties.

In an asynchronous teaching situation, other than tracking logins and grading submitted assignments, it's nearly impossible to know if students are watching recorded lectures at all or fast-forwarding to the end. Some districts use draconian measures such as requiring all personal laptops to have monitoring software during coursework, in some cases including webcam monitoring. However, even such severe measures are trivial to work around. It's not difficult to be watching a different video on a phone set next to the laptop.

It's nearly impossible to instill classroom discipline to the same degree in an online setting as a physical classroom. Sending someone to after-school detention or even suspending them isn't quite the same when the student is already staying at home. The line between truancy and poor performance also blurs. What's to keep an unmotivated student from logging in and ignoring the coursework if he isn't concerned with grades?

Parental oversight can go a long way in making sure that students are held accountable. Sending home a set of guidelines or expectations for the distance learning environment, or better yet, having a parent or guardian login to the LMS to provide an additional layer of oversight can be quite helpful at times. However, expect a wide range of commitment levels from parents, not just the students. In the end, there's little that can be done beyond a parent-teacher phone call or meeting to address truancy or discipline issues, other than warning of a failing grade. Be sure to follow all district guidelines on confidentiality and privacy for any parent-teacher communications.

Still, it's a good idea to involve the parents, even more so than you might ordinarily, for an online teaching module, particularly with younger students. You'll want to make sure that everyone has access to adequate equipment and resources. If there are special circumstances, like a noisy home environment with small toddlers, you'll want to work with the parents, and possibly the district, in finding a suitable solution, whether that involves lending equipment or providing isolated classrooms or library space for students in need.

Beyond parental involvement, grades are the primary form of accountability. For a physical classroom, homework assignments and exam scores are the most common components of a grade, with the occasional participation points and group projects added into the mix. The social constructs and disciplinary responses within a physical classroom are typically enough to enforce model behavior in the majority of students.

Don't expect the same in a virtual classroom. Even many adults struggle to adapt to a work-from-home environment. Create more leverage points for grading and other kinds of rewards. Create more accountability, as we'll describe in the next section.

Live stream a meeting With zoom

Setting up Live Streams

An option for holding massive virtual public events, webinars allow between 100-10,000 view-only participants. This means they can use the chat feature to ask questions if enabled but cannot speak directly and aren't as likely to interact with one another. Depending on chat settings, they may not interact with one another at all. You can have a further 100 panelists on top of this - participants who can speak and use their cameras. Webinars are only available to those with a Pro account or higher who have also purchased the Webinar add-on and can only be used by users who have been licensed. You can then, as the account Owner or Admin, assign the add-on to one of your Account users by signing into Zoom's website, then going to "User Management," then to "Users." Click "Edit" at the end of the Username that you wish to assign the license to, then ensure that "Licensed," then "Webinar" is ticked. Then, click "Save."

To set up a webinar, stay logged into the Zoom website, then go to "Webinars," then "Schedule a Webinar." You'll see the process is much like scheduling a meeting, and you'll even see the option to make your webinars recurring. By this point, you should be able to choose the options you want on or off without hand-holding.

Note that if you require participants to register, you can have them answer a pre-meeting questionnaire. You can do this via the Zoom web portal by going Webinars > Invitations > Approval > Edit, then navigating to the "Questions" and "Custom Questions" tabs. Do not forget to save when you're done. You can add your panelists while under "Invitations" too, by clicking on its own "Edit" button. Non-panelists are invited simply through the "Copy the invitation" and "Email me the invitation" options next to your webinar's name.

Once your webinar is set up, you can start it via Zoom's website, or your Zoom app through logging in, going under "Meetings," then finding your webinar and clicking "Start."

Aside from the addition of panelists and the potentially huge attendee sizes, Webinars have many of the features present in normal Zoom meetings. Consider using Mute All, Co-Hosts, and participant size add-ons as alternatives if you aren't sure a Webinar is what you need for your strategy. Note that there are no Reactions, Waiting Room, or File Transfer features in a Zoom webinar.

Live Streams

Live streaming is a feature that lets your Zoom meeting broadcast in real-time to other media platforms, allowing you to reach audiences on YouTube, Facebook, and more. Live streams can be enabled for both regular meetings and webinars, but again require an account of Pro or higher. To ensure live-streaming has been enabled for you, as an admin you can log onto Zoom's website and go Account Management > Account Settings > In Meeting (Advanced) > "Allow live-streaming the meetings."

Then, check the streaming services you wish to be able to use. For webinars, this can be done via the Account Management > Webinar Settings > Edit. If you wish to use a custom streaming service, be sure to check that option, then provide a Stream URL, a Page URL, and a Stream Key where you're prompted for instructions, so hosts will be able to use that custom option should they wish.

Then, when you wish to host a live-streaming meeting, log into Zoom's website. Click on "Meetings." Then, schedule a new meeting. When you click "Save," investigate the Advanced Options that pop up. You'll see which platforms your meeting will be able to stream to, as well as for instructions for how to commence live streaming in your Zoom app. If you wish to use a custom service, click on "configure live stream settings" now. This will let you fill in the Stream URL, Page URL, and Stream Key for your customer service now, so you won't need to worry about doing so when trying to live stream mid-meeting.

Tips for live stream zoom

There are a few things you can do to ensure you have the best experience when incorporating video conferencing into your workflow.

Proper Lighting

It's important to ensure that your location is properly lit when using video communication to ensure your video recipient can see you. It can involve getting away from windows that can induce backlighting whether they're behind you or shadows are intense. Likewise, low light can be a problem, so be sure to have overhead lighting or a handy lamp to fight low sunlight.

Invest in the best quality headphones

In a quiet home environment, depending on your computer speakers and microphone capability may be adequate. This might not always be the case in a large office, coworking room, even whether you have to answer a call when out and about. There are plenty of decent ones on the market and that could be the difference between a smooth video chat and a boring one where everyone needs to repeat themselves over and over again.

Preliminary Troubleshooting

Have a couple of tried and tested troubleshooting solutions available as problems inevitably emerge. Your Internet protection tools, for example, could block your webcam or audio. Or the headphones which you use may not produce the best quality of audio. Know where your preferences for configurations are for applications that you use to search for quick fixes such as unselecting options that obstruct access to audio or webcams.

Still have right to back up

Although technological requirements are increasingly growing, technology still has a way to fail right as its most important. For those who cannot use their machines for any purpose, Zoom helps you to dial into video calls from a landline. You may also have other favored forms of backup.

CHAPTER 4:

How To Use Zoom For Webinars

Most Zoom users will be using the service for meetings but there will be other users who will use the webinar feature of Zoom for personal or business reasons.

Webinars are invaluable in gathering a group of people that can't be together for the sake of workshops and impromptu meetings.

It makes it possible for such activities to occur like they were all there.

Zoom has taken the lead in making these activities possible

It's noteworthy to understand what a webinar is; A Webinar refers to an online event where a speaker or more addresses a large audience on a particular topic of interest. Webinars give the host a level of control over such meetings via enhanced features.

Zoom webinar services can accommodate a 100-10,000 person audience. To activate your webinar service, you have to choose any of the zoom plans that you can afford and buy the webinar add-on to be able to subscribe to the webinar services. The zoom plan subscribed to determines the number of people that can attend the meeting

Having been licensed by Zoom, you can proceed to put your webinar in shape

Highlight the Webinar option in the Personal section of the Zoom icon, schedule a webinar button will pop up, select it

After that, fill in the topic for the webinar, elucidate what the webinar would entail, and signify when it will take place.

Interestingly, there's room for webinars occurring periodically, to get this done, click on the Recurring webinar bar, you then get to decide how often it will occur, the time it should take place, and also the date when it should end.

Additional checkmates can be introduced to streamline your audience. Having a period when your audience is expected to register before a set deadline and then given a password that grants them access to the webinar via the specified gadget, you also reserve the right to decide if the host/hosts can be seen during the webinar.

Furthermore, you can choose to create opportunities for questions and answers, if the option is enabled, attendees can get to see the questions, or it's made anonymous

To access the webinar Q&A settings, scroll to Webinar Option, click Q&A, and select Schedule

Alternative hosts have the permission to oversee meetings in your stead once they receive the link via a notification email however scheduling of meetings is your responsibility.

You can save this event to your Google calendar using the confirmation page. Towards the end of the confirmation page, you'll see an invitation bar that enables you to incorporate your panelists, feed them with details of the event that are disseminated to your attendees

From the email settings tab, you can determine the arrangement of emails to be sent to panelists and attendees before the event as reminders and as follow-up messages when the event is over.

You can decide to add flavor to your zoom webinar by adding colorful logos/designs to invitations sent to your attendees

Registering attendees for zoom webinar

Under Invite Attendees, click edit. You can ask your attendees to register using a form or submit their biodata {name and email address}. Approval can be done manual or otherwise automatic. Your choice of registration should depend largely on your intention, if you have plans to follow your attendees up after the webinar/do a survey, you can ask questions that will enable you to know more about them

How to register attendees for a Zoom webinar with JotForm:
After setting up your webinar, locking down your co-hosts, it remains pertinent to get people to attend your event; hence you have to make sure attendees signing up do this without glitches

This is where Jotform comes in. It provides a glitch-free way of extracting data from attendees and it enables you to fashion the questions to suit your taste. It also allows you to sell your company value/culture through making customized designs in the form off course although templates are available, and it gives you the leverage to determine to an extent the response intended from your attendees

During the registration, attendees can be asked for relevant information such as their occupation, company name, address; it can be made compulsory before attendees sign up for your webinar

Once the attendees complete the filling of the form, they are verified automatically. This form can also be linked to several online payment platforms hence registration fees can be collected for these webinars. There are no hidden charges; hence only standard charges apply to these payment platforms are deducted

If you chose the option of automatic approval, you can just take a chill pill and watch your attendee base surge but if you opted for manual approval, you have to log in to the zoom app and manually approve those that filled the Jotform

How to enable registration for a Zoom webinar
To ensure people register, enable the register bar which is found under the personal section of your zoom portal and the webinar tab, this cannot be overemphasized and should be credence even before data collection, however, if the webinar has already been scheduled, it can be edited by selecting the already archived webinar under the 'Upcoming webinar' tab

Towards the end of the page, select Edit this Webinar, this takes you back to the menu where you can enable registration ab-initio.

How to use zoom for online meetings

Online meetings are sometimes used interchangeably with Webinars. No doubt, similarities exist but there are also differences between the two

Webinars are designed to accommodate a larger group of people as opposed to an online meeting where there are usually fewer participants

Online meetings are more collaborative and give the participants a great deal of control; there's the freedom to screen-share, deliberate on matters arising whereas in webinars, opinions are aired through question and answer, only the host/ co-hosts are the ones that do the talking.

Going into the nitty-gritty, let's talk about how to use Zoom for online meetings

To help you out, here's a step-by-step guide to using Zoom Meetings the right way.

We'll cover the steps for both desktop and mobile platforms on:

- How to Set Up a Zoom Meeting
- How to Join a Zoom Meeting
- How to Schedule Meetings
- How to Record Meetings
- How to Set Up a Zoom Meeting

Here's a step-by-step guide to set up a Zoom meeting easily:

For Desktop

To start a zoom meeting, log in to your zoom account, select the 'Host a meeting' tab, the following options will surface: With Video on, With Video off, and screen share only, choose the appropriate option

You will be redirected to the zoom app where the meeting can start, here you can take note of the invitation URL that attendees will need to gain access to the meeting

To invite your participants, select the Invite button in the new meeting screen. You get the option of inviting your participants using a URL or Invitation, this can be sent via an instant message, email, or text

An email containing the meeting details can be sent to the participants via your chosen email client

pag. 272

For Mobile Devices
Log into your zoom app, click the 'New meeting' icon, edit the meeting settings in line with the options that suit you. After that, click on the 'Start a Meeting' button. To add participants, tap the 'Participants' icon once the meeting starts, once the participant menu opens up, select the Invite tab. Then, you can share the meeting details through email, text, instant messages

How to Join a Zoom Meeting

You can join using a meeting link or a meeting ID

Join Using a Meeting Link

To join using a meeting link, click on the link or if using a web browser, copy and paste

Join Using A Meeting ID

Log into your zoom app, select the Join button, input the meeting ID and your display name for the meeting, tap the 'Join' button

You can now start your meeting with your partners

How to Schedule Meetings

Important meetings can be forgotten when you have a tight schedule

With Zoom, however, you can schedule meetings beforehand to avoid this. This can be done by setting its date and time, providing a meeting ID, ascertaining whether it needs a password to join or not. The steps to scheduling meetings are hereby laid down:

For Desktop
Go to the zoom app and tap on the 'Schedule button'. Next, you input the meeting details in the 'Schedule meeting' icon that appears. Its data and time, privacy, and access setting can be inputted.

When you're done making adjustments, tap the schedule button at the bottom right of the screen

For Mobile
Log into the Zoom app, go to the meet and chat page, and select Schedule. Input the meeting name, time, and date, then tap done. You can save this to your calendar as a reminder

How to Record Zoom Meetings

This feature allows you to document meetings in virtual form and it's indispensable in groups who use zoom as their major tool for communication

These recordings can be saved to your device or Zoom cloud where every member of the team can access it

Here's how to record Zoom meetings:

For Desktop
Once the meeting starts, click on the 'Record' icon, you'll have two options, to record on the computer or to record to the cloud, to stop the recording, simply click on Pause/stop recording, alternatively, ending the meeting automatically stops the recording. After the meeting, the recording can be saved to your preferred storage and archived where it can be retrieved at any point in time.

For Mobile
On mobile devices, Zoom lets you save meeting recordings only to the Zoom Cloud. Here's how to record a Zoom meeting from your mobile: Here, you only have the option of saving recordings to zoom cloud. Once the meeting starts, click on the 'More' option, select the 'Record to the cloud' to begin recording, you can pause or stop recording by tapping the 'More' button, after the meeting, the recording is saved to the folder 'My Recordings.

Scheduling a Webinar

To schedule a Zoom webinar, you will need to sign in to the web interface and then go to the Webinars section and click on **Schedule a Webinar**.

- **Description** – If you want to add a description of what your webinar will be covering then you can do so here.
- **When** – This is the start date of the webinar.
- **Duration** – This is how long the webinar is scheduled to run. You can end it early or have it run longer if needed.
- **Time Zone** – If you need to change the time zone to something different than what your computer is set to then you can do so here. If you check the box for **Recurring webinar** then you will be able to schedule your webinar to re-run at specific times using the same webinar ID.
- **Webinar Password** – You can require your participants to enter a password to get into your webinar if you are concerned about security.
- **Video** – Here you can decide if you want your participant's video to automatically start when they enter your room.
- **Webinar Options** – There are several additional options you can choose from here to fine-tune your webinar experience.
- **Q&A** – This allows attendees to ask questions during the webinar that can be answered by the panelists, co-hosts, and the host.
- **Enable Practice Session** – This allows you and your panelists to get set up and familiarized with the Zoom webinar controls before you go live with your webinar.
- **Only authenticated users can join** – If you want to make your account more secure then you can set up authenticated users in your account management and then only those who have been configured will be able to join your webinars.

- **Record the webinar automatically** – Use this option if you want Zoom to record your webinar automatically without you needing to start it manually.

Once you have configured all of your webinar options then click the Schedule button to have the webinar listed in your upcoming webinars.

Templates

If you have spent some time configuring your webinar to get it just the way you like it then you might want to consider saving it as a template so you can use it over again for another webinar.

To save a current webinar as a template simply go to the settings for that webinar and click on the link that says **Save this webinar as a template**.

Then you can give the template a name and decide if you would like to save the recurrences of the webinar within the template.

Once you name the template click on the **Save as Template** button to have it saved to your Zoom account.

Now when you go to your **Webinar Templates** under Webinars in the web interface you will see your newly saved template that you can then click on and use to schedule a new webinar using its saved settings.

Branding

Branding is a way to customize your webinar experience by adding things such as banners, logos, and themes to your webinar that enhances the overall look and feel of your presentation.

You can start the branding process by going to the webinar section, selecting a webinar, and then clicking the Branding section.

pag. 276

The various options in the Branding section and then show some examples.

Title – This information will be displayed at the top middle section of the page.

Banner – You can create your custom banner and save it as an image file to be used in your webinar.

Logo – If you have a company logo that you want to have displayed during your webinar then you can upload it from here.

Speakers – Many times you will have additional people who will be speaking during your webinar. You can upload their photo and additional information about these people in this section.

Theme – Zoom offers several different color schemes that you can choose from if you want to change the way your overall webinar looks.

Post Attendee URL – This section can be used to add a website for your company or that your attendees can go to for additional information about whatever you might be discussing in your webinar.

Post Webinar Survey – If you use any type of survey site and have set up a survey about your webinar then you can add the site address here.

Social Media Share Description – Here you can enter the description that you would like to be included when the webinar is shared on Facebook or LinkedIn and also decide if you want to include your uploaded logo or banner.

I have gone through the above settings and did things such as add a banner, logo, speaker, and post attendee URL.

You will see how these apply to my webinar when it's time to start it.

Configuring Polls

Polls are a great way to get information from your attendees by asking them a question or series of questions about your webinar. You can choose from a single choice answer or a multiple-choice answer.

To get to the poll settings, simply go to your webinar and then the **Polls** section and click the **Add** button and add a question. Next, you will need to select if you want to use a single choice question or a multiple-choice question. I will use a multiple-choice question for my example and ask if anyone is interested in buying my book after hearing about it in my webinar and give them three answers to choose from.

Conclusion

Now that you have learned everything about Zoom you can now start using it in your online classes or online meetings, especially now that we are avoiding going out and meeting other people due to the going ongoing pandemic, Zoom is a big help in solving our problems. Zoom is not just about a mere video call but has many features as well such as sharing your screen, sending a file, creating polls, a delegation of duties, muting/unmuting, keyboard shortcuts, as well as safety measures to avoid Zoom bombing. This does not only help us during these times, but we can always use this during future events that require convenience and safety. I hope that you will remember everything that was discussed here because this will be very helpful in our online classes and online meetings, don't forget to be creative by changing your virtual background and many more you can explore.

This book talks a lot about technology, but it is primarily about teaching and learning. There are many ways to teach and many ways to learn. Some modalities will be more effective in some kinds of learning than others, and within each modality, some strategies are more effective than others in preparing students with the knowledge and skills to be successful in their future lives. Technology is providing an increasingly widening variety of tools that allow teachers to create that learning experience at a distance in ways that can be equally effective in developing successful learners as classroom instruction. It is all about using these tools appropriately.

But technology does not replace the teacher. Regardless of how many tools you throw at a course, its success depends upon the students' willingness and capacity to engage with the course activities. Good teachers have always known that. You as the teacher make the decisions on how the technology will be used to engage your students with the content, with you, and their classmates. In a course that combines videoconferencing and an LMS, you have the strengths of both synchronous and asynchronous tools that allow you to engage your students both during and outside of class in a variety of modes that just are not possible in the traditional classroom format alone.

The consensus of research demonstrates that distance education can be as effective in meeting learning goals as classroom-based education. It just takes more work. I am confident that this work is worth the effort, however, because with distance technologies the reach of your knowledge and skills as a teacher goes far beyond a school campus. It can span the globe, bringing together international perspectives that enrichen everyone who participates. I am confident that the deep investigation into all aspects of your course teaches you that teaching in these new modalities will expand your world too, forcing you to look at teaching and learning in new ways, perhaps improving both your distance and classroom teaching. I wish you the best on your journey ahead!

It is recommended that you keep this book handy as you go, for the time being, spending the next few months always turning back to it to revise its advice, although as you grow more and more advanced, and as Zoom gains more and more updates, you'll increasingly find a potent companion in the company's website, where you can learn all about its latest features and how to work with specific devices.

However, no matter what changes, Zoom will likely remain a socially sensitive and user-friendly application, reinforcing Eric Yuan's dream of helping young lovers look into each other's eyes without having to wait a whole month or endure a grueling 10-hour train ride.

This is likely why even the free version allows you to hold a conversation for eternity when it's kept small and intimate. For those who do not need to hold massive meetings with their division or department, but just want to see the faces of their family again, Zoom still has them covered.

And yet, for those whose interests are professionally inclined, zoom carries nearly every feature you could want in delivering a compelling talk to scores of people at a time, each one of whom could be connecting from anywhere in the world.

This could be you, doing all these things, right now. Potentially for free. Whatever you decide to do from this point, I hope Zoom helps make the process easier for you, whether you're trying to land your next interview, host a long-awaited reunion or set up your own small business to stay afloat and realize your dreams.

Printed in Great Britain
by Amazon